THE SPIRIT OF ZEN

THE SPIRIT OF ZEN

*A way of life, work and art
in the Far East*

ALAN W. WATTS

GROVE PRESS, INC. NEW YORK

First Evergreen Edition 1960
Twentieth Printing 1980
ISBN: 0-394-17418-6
Grove Press ISBN: 0-8021-4113-7
Library of Congress Catalog Card Number: 60-7347

Manufactured in the United States of America

Distributed by Random House, Inc., New York

GROVE PRESS, INC., 196 West Houston Street, New York, N.Y. 10014

To
Christmas Humphreys

Contents

Preface to the Third Edition

The appearance of a third edition of this work has given me the opportunity to make some further changes to improve its accuracy. Though I am still somewhat unsatisfied with the general presentation of Mahayana philosophy in the first chapter, I found that a complete rewriting of this section would so disrupt the artistic integrity of the book that I should have to rewrite almost the entire work. The bibliography has been brought up to date, but it is no longer exhaustive.

ALAN W. WATTS

Mill Valley, California
June, 1958

Preface to the First Edition

I should never have been able to write this book if it had not been for the work of Professor Daisetz Teitaro Suzuki of the Otani Buddhist College at Kyoto. It is to him that we of the West owe almost all our knowledge of Zen, and I am deeply grateful to him for his permission to quote from many of his translations of the writings and sayings of Zen masters which appear in the following pages. This book will be to some their first introduction to Zen, and I strongly advise them to turn afterwards to the three volumes of Professor Suzuki's *Essays in Zen Buddhism*, where they will find the subject treated in the fullest way.

I must also give special thanks to Mr Christmas Humphreys, President of the Buddhist Lodge, London, for reading through my manuscript and making many valuable suggestions for its improvement. Indeed, I owe him further thanks, for it was he who not only introduced me to the work of Professor Suzuki but laid the foundations of my knowledge of Buddhism. For this I can never be sufficiently grateful.

ALAN W. WATTS

Bromley, Kent
December, 1935

Preface to the Second Edition

Since this book was first written, nearly twenty years ago, I have been enabled to learn a great deal more, and in some ways a great deal less, about Zen Buddhism. Since 1935 a large amount of new information about Zen has become available. Not only has Dr D. T. Suzuki published some five or six new works, but a number of other authors—notably R. H. Blyth and Eugen Herrigel—have written important works from their first-hand experience. Fresh information of a more strictly academic type has also become available through the labours of Hu Shih, Fung Yu-lan, Jacques Gernet, Heinrich Dumoulin, and several others. Furthermore, I have had the privilege, denied to me before writing this book, of many conversations with Japanese exponents of Zen, including Dr Suzuki himself, Sokei-an Sasaki, Nyogen Senzaki, and Sohaku Ogata.

Perhaps as a result of the last-mentioned opportunity, I may be said to know a bit less about Zen than in 1935. For living Zen, as distinct from academic Zen, is above all a process of unlearning, of the abandonment of ideology, of all fixed forms of thought and feeling whereby the mind tries to grasp its own life. Thus I do not really know what Zen is, because Zen—the essential experience underlying Buddhism—is not a 'what'. It is not a *thing*, which is to say an aspect of experience definable by a word or concept. Zen is closer to what Korzybski has called the 'unspeakable' level of reality—the non-verbal, non-symbolic, and totally indefinable world of the concrete as distinct from the abstract. For all things, whether objects or processes, are abstracted from experience by thinking and naming. As Buddhism said so many centuries before semantics and metalinguistics, 'Originally not one thing exists.'

Therefore a book which purports to explain Zen is something of a hoax in the respect that the more it succeeds in giving the reader an impression of intelligibility, the more it has failed to give understanding. A proper exposition of Zen should 'tease us out of thought', and leave the mind like an open window instead of a panel of stained glass.

The only important change in this second edition is that it carries a completely new bibliography, which is, I believe, as complete a list of writings of Zen in European languages as may be found. This is an important feature of a book which was never intended to be anything more than a popular introduction to Zen, and made no claims to originality or depth of scholarship. Any major changes in the body of the text would have been too expensive, though I would have liked to rewrite the discussion of Mahayana philosophy in the first chapter and to modify much of what was said about the *koan*. Some years of the study of Chinese would also have tempted me to retranslate a number of quotations and technical phrases. I would also like to have given the alternative account of the history of the introduction of Zen into China proposed by Hu Shih and Fung Yu-lan, which takes it back to Tao-sheng (A.D. 360-434), and regards the Bodhidharma story as somewhat legendary.

In conclusion, I would like to say something about the present state of the study of Zen in the Western world. In the past fifteen years or so, it has become very widely known in Europe and America, and is exercising a great intellectual and artistic influence. It is most gratifying that it has not, to any important extent, become a new fad in religious cults, with organizations seeking converts. Happily, Zen finds its place in the West as a study of serious interest for three principal groups.

In philosophical circles it is being found of special relevance to those who are looking for a step beyond the important insights of logical positivism and scientific empiricism. For Western philosophy seemed to have reached a point of *impasse*, at which it must either 'close up shop' or break loose from the vicious circle of verbal speculation. Among scientists, its interest has been chiefly for psychotherapists and for students of the new sciences of language—semantics and metalinguistics. Not only are the states of mind involved in Zen-practice of great psychological interest, but their ways of releasing thought and action from vicious circles suggest many practical applications.

In the world of art, the influence of Zen is more indirect, and is seen in the great indebtedness of contemporary architecture and ceramics in the United States to Japanese feelings for space and texture. One should not forget to mention, also, the work of the potter Bernard Leach in England, nor to remember that nearly thirty years ago Georges Duthuit called attention to this trend in his *Chinese Mysticism and Modern Painting*.

But in all these instances it is not quite correct to say that a 'Zen influence' is simply being imported and imitated. It is rather a case of deep answering to deep, of tendencies already implicit in Western life which leap into actuality through an outside stimulus. So far as Zen is concerned, this must always be the way, for as a verse in the *Zenrin Kushu* says:

> If you do not get it from yourself,
> Where will you go for it?

ALAN W. WATTS

San Francisco, 1954

Foreword

A short time ago Zen Buddhism was almost entirely unknown to the West, with the exception of a few Orientalists whose interest in the subject was primarily academic. Before the First World War there was only one work on Zen in any European language—Kaiten Nukariya's *Religion of the Samurai*—and a few scattered references in books on Buddhism in general. It was not until Professor D. T. Suzuki of Kyoto published the first volume of his *Essays in Zen Buddhism* in 1927 that there was any work presented so as to excite the interest of the West with any effect, and at the same time to convey something of the real spirit of Zen. Subsequently Professor Suzuki published two more volumes of *Essays*, and it is largely owing to his work that we know anything of the subject at all. The result of his labours has been a swiftly increasing interest in Zen, not confined only to professed students of Oriental philosophy. Zen is so markedly different from any other form of Buddhism, one might even say from any other form of religion, that it has roused the curiosity of many who would not ordinarily look to the 'unpractical' East for practical wisdom.

Once that curiosity is aroused it is not easily set at rest, for Zen has a peculiar fascination for minds weary of conventional religion and philosophy. From the start Zen dispenses with all forms of theorization, doctrinal instruction and lifeless formality; these are treated as the mere symbols of wisdom, and Zen is founded on practice and on an intimate, personal experience of the reality to which most forms of religion and philosophy come no nearer than an intellectual or emotional

description. That is not to say that Zen is the only true path
to Enlightenment; it has been said that the difference between
Zen and other forms of religion is that 'all other paths wind
slowly up the mountain-side, but Zen, like a Roman road,
thrusts all obstacles aside and moves in a direct line to the
Goal'. After all, creeds, dogmas and philosophical systems are
only ideas *about* the truth, in the same way as words are not
facts but only *about* facts, whereas Zen is a vigorous attempt
to come into direct contact with the truth itself without allowing theories and symbols to stand between the knower and the
known. In a certain sense Zen is feeling life instead of feeling
something *about* life; it has no patience with second-hand wisdom, with someone else's description of a spiritual experience,
or with mere conceptions and beliefs. While second-hand
wisdom is valuable as a signpost pointing the way, it is too
easily taken for the path itself or even for the goal. So subtle
are the ways in which descriptions of truth may pose as truth
itself that Zen is often a form of iconoclasm, a breaking down
of the mere intellectual images of the living reality, knowable
only by personal experience.

But it is in its methods of instruction that Zen is unique.
There is no doctrinal teaching, no study of scriptures, no
formal programme of spiritual development. Apart from a
few collections of sermons by the earlier Zen masters, which
are the only attempts at a *rational* exposition of its teachings,
almost the whole of our records of Zen instruction are a
number of dialogues (*mondo*) between the masters and their
disciples which seem to pay so little attention to the usual
standards of logic and sound reasoning as to appear at first
sight to be nonsense. There are a number of commentaries
upon these dialogues, and a large collection of short poems
such as are found in Chinese and Japanese pictures, but from

Foreword

the intellectual standpoint these have little more meaning than the dialogues themselves. So baffling are these records that Wieger could only describe Zen literature as 'nombre d'infolio remplis de réponses incohérentes, insensées . . . Ce ne sont pas, comme on l'a supposé, des allusions à des affaires intérieures, qu'il faudrait connaître pour pouvoir comprendre. Ce sont des exclamations échappées à des abrutis, momentanément tirés de leur coma.'

But it is easy to be led astray by outward appearances, and just as the highest and the lowest notes are equally inaudible, so, perhaps, is the greatest sense and the greatest nonsense equally unintelligible. But Zen does not attempt to be intelligible, that is to say, capable of being understood by the intellect. The method of Zen is to baffle, excite, puzzle and exhaust the intellect until it is realized that intellection is only thinging *about*; it will provoke, irritate and again exhaust the emotions until it is realized that emotion is only feeling *about*, and then it contrives, when the disciple has been brought to an intellectual and emotional impasse, to bridge the gap between second-hand, conceptual contact with reality, and first-hand experience. To effect this it calls into play a higher faculty of the mind, known as intuition or *Buddhi*, which is sometimes called the 'Eye of the Spirit'. In short, the aim of Zen is to focus the attention on reality itself, instead of on our intellectual and emotional reactions to reality—reality being that ever-changing, ever-growing, indefinable something known as 'life', which will never stop for a moment for us to fit it satisfactorily into any rigid system of pigeon-holes and ideas.

Thus anyone who attempts to write about Zen has to encounter unusual difficulties; he can never explain, he can only indicate; he can only go on setting problems and giving hints which at best can bring the reader tantalizingly nearer to the truth, but the moment he attempts any fixed definition the thing slips away, and the definition is seen to be no more than a philosophical conception. Zen cannot be made to fit into any '-ism' or '-ology'; it is alive and cannot be dissected and analysed like a corpse. Therefore, if we have any doubts about the sense and sanity of the sayings of the Zen masters, let us, to begin with, give them the benefit of the doubt, and assume that there is wisdom in their complete disregard for logic. For instance, master Wu Tsu says, 'Let me take an illustration from a fable. A cow passes through a window. Its head, horns, and the four legs pass over easily, but only the tail cannot pass through. Why can't it?' Or again, a monk came to master Chao-chou and asked, 'I have just come to this monastery. Would you mind giving me some instruction, please?' The master said, 'Have you eaten your breakfast yet, or not?' 'Yes, I have, sir.' 'Then wash your bowls.' It is said that as a result of this conversation the monk became enlightened.

Whether this is madness or not, the fact remains that Zen has profoundly influenced the whole culture of the Far East, and it is by its translation into thought and action that we must test the value of the inward spirit, however incomprehensible it may seem. Westerners must often have wondered how the great artistic achievements of the Far East have obtained that subtle and indefinable quality which gives them a unique place among the creations of the human spirit. The answer is that it comes from Zen—a way of life whose vital part in the history of Chinese and Japanese civilization has, until recent years, been much underestimated, for it is only recently that we have been given any clue as to what Zen itself is.

The Origins of Zen

Just as it is impossible to explain the beauty of a sunset to a man blind from his birth, so is it impossible for sages to find any words which will express their wisdom to men of lesser understanding. For the wisdom of sages is not in their teachings; otherwise anybody might become a sage simply by reading the *Bhagavad-Gita*, the *Dialogues* of Plato or the Buddhist Scriptures. As it is, one may study these books for a lifetime without being any the wiser, for to seek Enlightenment in words and ideas (to borrow a phrase from Dr Trigant Burrow) is like expecting 'the sight of a menu-card to reach and satisfy the inner processes of a hungry man'. Nothing, however, is easier than to confuse the wisdom of a sage with his doctrine, for in the absence of any understanding of truth another man's description of his understanding is easily mistaken for truth itself. Yet it is no more truth than a signpost is the town to which it points. Gautama the *Buddha* (Enlightened One) was careful to avoid any descriptions of the illumination which he found while sitting one night under a giant fig-tree at Gaya, and we are told that when he was questioned upon the ultimate mysteries of the universe he 'maintained a noble silence'. He never tired of saying that his doctrine (Dharma) was concerned only with the Way to Enlightenment, and he never claimed it as a *revelation* of Enlightenment. Hence the Buddhist verse:

When they curiously question thee, seeking to know what It is,
Do not affirm anything, and do not deny anything.

21

For whatsoever is affirmed is not true,
And whatsoever is denied is not true.
How shall anyone say truly what That may be
While he has not himself fully won to What Is?
And, after he has won, what word is to be sent from a Region
Where the chariot of speech finds no track on which to go?
Therefore, to their questionings offer them silence only,
Silence—and a finger pointing the Way.

Even so, the followers of the Buddha have sought Enlightenment in that finger instead of going whither it points into the silence; they have revered and depended upon the records of his sayings as if they enshrined his wisdom, yet in so doing they have made those records not only a shrine but the tomb in which the dead carcass of his wisdom is buried. Enlightenment, however, is living and cannot be fixed down into any form of words; therefore the object of the Zen School of Buddhism is to go beyond words and ideas in order that the original insight of the Buddha may be brought back to life. It regards this insight as the one important thing; scriptures are no more than devices, mere temporary expedients, for showing where it may be found. It never makes the mistake of confusing teachings with wisdom, for essentially, Zen is that 'something' which makes the difference between a Buddha and an ordinary man; it is Enlightenment as distinct from doctrine.

Like so many of the key words of Oriental philosophy, 'Zen' has no exact equivalent in English. It is a Japanese word, derived from the Chinese *Ch'an* or *Ch'an-na* which is in turn a transliteration of the Sanskrit *Dhyana*, usually translated as 'meditation'. This is a misleading translation because to the Englishman 'meditation' means little more than deep thought and reflection, whereas in Yoga psychology *Dhyana* is a high

state of consciousness in which man finds union with the Ultimate Reality of the universe. The same is true of *Ch'an* and Zen, except that the Chinese mentality preferred to find this union less through solitary meditation in the jungle than through the work of everyday life. There is nothing 'other-wordly' about Zen, for it is a constant attitude of mind just as applicable to washing clothes as to performing religious offices, and whereas the Yogi retires from the world to achieve his *Dhyana*, Zen is found in a monastic community where master and disciples share all the work of supporting the monastery —growing rice, gardening, cooking, chopping wood and keeping the place clean. Thus if 'Zen' is to be translated at all, the nearest equivalent is 'Enlightenment', but even so Zen is not only Enlightenment; it is also the way to its attainment.

There is a tradition that Zen originated at the moment when the Buddha attained his supreme insight into the mysteries of life that night at Gaya in the Fifth Century B.C. That insight was handed down through a line of twenty-eight Patriarchs until it came to a certain Bodhidharma, who brought Zen to China in the Sixth Century A.D. Legends say that this insight was passed from one to the other without any intermediary of scriptures or doctrinal teaching; it was a 'direct transmission', a communication which passed immediately from mind to mind, understandable only by that person who was far enough developed to grasp his master's Enlightenment. While this 'Secret Message' was being carried on, the followers of the Buddha were forming themselves into many different sects, which fell into two main divisions—the Mahayana (Greater Vehical of the Law) and the Hinayana (Lesser Vehicle), the latter being a term of contempt invented by the adherents of the former. The difference between the two was largely the result of a dispute over the authority of certain sets of

The Origins of Zen

scriptures. None of the Buddha's teachings was committed to writing until at least 150 years after his death; until that time they were repeated from memory and so were given a tabulated and mechanical form particularly unattractive to the Western student. The inevitable result was that they became full of monkish interpolations (see Mrs Rhys Davids' *Outline of Buddhism*), and though it is generally assumed that the Pali version is more original than the Sanskrit scriptures of the Mahayana, there is little doubt that even these have wandered far from the actual words of the Buddha. The Hinayana or Theravada (Way of the Elders) is composed of those who accept only the Pali version, known as the Tipitaka (the Three Baskets). So convinced are they that this version contains the last word of the Buddha's wisdom that they refuse to recognize any ideas or precepts which it does not include, and because its instructions are largely concerned with matters of conduct, the psycho-physical analysis of man, and the monastic regimen, the Hinayana has become a formal and rigid, almost materialistic, school of thought. From the time of its origin to the present day its philosophy has neither changed nor grown in any important respect. The Sanskrit scriptures of the Mahayana, on the other hand, are composed chiefly of metaphysical discourses, which were continually elaborated and subjected again and again to fresh interpretations. Geographically, the Hinayana is confined to the southern part of Asia—Ceylon, Burma and Siam—while the Mahayana went northwards to China, Tibet, Mongolia, Korea and Japan. Whereas the Hinayana does not differ importantly from country to country, the Mahayana embraces a number of distinct sects, ranging from the highly ritualistic Lamaism of Tibet to the fresh simplicity of Zen in Japan.

Both Hinayana and Mahayana Buddhism have a common

basis in the elementary principles of the Buddha's doctrine. Briefly, this doctrine is that man suffers because of his craving to possess and keep for ever things which are essentially impermanent. Chief among these things is his own person, for this is his means of isolating himself from the rest of life, his castle into which he can retreat and from which he can assert himself against external forces. He believes that this fortified and isolated position is the best means of obtaining happiness; it enables him to fight against change, to strive to keep pleasing things for himself, to shut out suffering and to shape circumstances as he wills. In short, it is his means of resisting life. The Buddha taught that all things, including this castle, are essentially impermanent and that as soon as man tries to possess them they slip away; this frustration of the desire to possess is the immediate cause of suffering. But he went further than this, for he showed that the fundamental cause is the delusion that man *can* isolate himself from life. A false isolation is achieved by identifying himself with his castle, the person, but because this castle is impermanent it has no abiding reality, it is empty of any 'self-nature' (*atta*) and is no more the Self than any other changing object. What, then, is the Self? The Buddha remained silent when asked this question, but he taught that man will find out only when he no longer identifies himself with his person, when he no longer resists the external world from within its fortification, in fact, when he makes an end of his hostility and his plundering expeditions against life. In contrast to this philosophy of isolation the Buddha proclaimed the unity of all living things and charged his followers to replace this hostility by divine compassion (*karuna*). The practice of this teaching brings the disciple to the state of Nirvana, the end of suffering and the extinction of selfishness, the condition of eternal bliss which

The Origins of Zen

no words can describe. In addition to this philosophy of life, the Buddha incorporated into his doctrine the ancient principles of Karma (the law of conditioned action) and its corollary Rebirth or Reincarnation (see Appendix II). These imply that death is no escape from suffering, for 'each man's life the outcome of his former living is'; death is only a temporary rest, and man must work out his own deliverance through numberless lives until he attains the final Enlightenment. However, few Zen Buddhists interpret the doctrine of rebirth quite so literally. To be reborn is rather to be under the illusion that a continuing ego survives from moment to moment, to feel that I who sit here am truly I who came in at the door ten minutes ago.

So far both Mahayana and Hinayana are in agreement, but they disagree over the Buddha's silence on the question of the Self. *What* is found when man no longer resists life from behind the barrier of his person? Because the Buddha denied the existence of any 'self-nature' in the person, the Hinayana takes this to mean that there is no Self at all. The Mahayana, on the other hand, considers that a true Self is found when the false one is renounced. When man neither identifies himself with his person nor uses it as a means of resisting life, he finds that the Self is more than his own being; it includes the whole universe. The Hinayana, realizing that no single thing as such is the Self, is content with that realization; hence it is a denial of life, conceiving Enlightenment only as the negative attainment of understanding that all separate entities are *anatta*—without self, and *anicca*—without permanence. But the Mahayana completes this denial with an affirmation; while denying the existence of self in any particular thing, it finds it in the total interrelatedness of all things. Thus Enlightenment is to deny the self in the castle, to realize that Self is not this

27

The Spirit of Zen

person called 'I' as distinct from that person called 'You', but that it is both 'I' and 'You' and everything else included. The Mahayana therefore affirms life by declaring that all things are the Self, instead of denying it by saying only that in each thing, taken separately, there is no self. Yet fundamentally there is no disagreement on this point between Mahayana and Hinayana; the difference is that the former goes further than the latter. Furthermore, Mahayana philosophy designates the true Self by the term *sunyata* or 'voidness' to show, not that it is merely nothing, but that it surpasses every idea which the mind can form. Reality cannot be grasped in the idea of Being, because Being is meaningless apart from Non-being, and *vice versa*. The true Self is not an idea but an experience —the experience which comes to pass when the mind has voided every metaphysical premise, every idea with which it attempts to grasp the nature of the world.

But this difference in theory gave rise to an important difference in practice. The Hinayanist, because of his negative ideal, regards the highest form of man as he who simply attains his Nirvana, his release, through the realization of *anatta* and *anicca*, and leaves it at that. Such a one is known as an Arhan as distinct from a Bodhisattva, the ideal man of Mahayana philosophy. Here is one who is not content with the mere attainment of Nirvana; the Bodhisattva feels that he cannot enjoy eternal bliss while other beings suffer, because he knows that there is no essential difference between them and himself, and his Nirvana cannot be complete if they do not share it. Because he affirms all life as the Self he regards all beings as his 'other selves', and for him Nirvana is a vanity and a selfishness if there is a single creature still unenlightened. Therefore after countless lives of painful striving against self-delusion he attains the right to eternal bliss, only to renounce it in order that he may work for the enlightenment of every living thing. The ideal of the Bodhisattva implies the most complete acceptance of life, for the Bodhisattva can exclude nothing and neglect nothing because he identifies himself with everything. 'Forgoing self, the universe grows I.' Therefore Keyserling describes him as he 'who says yes to the most evil world, for he knows himself to be one with it. Rid of himself, he feels his foundation in God, his surface, however, intertwined with everything which exists. Thus he must love all beings as he loves himself, thus he cannot rest until everyone mirrors the divinity in everything.'

In Mahayana philosophy this divinity, the Self, was known as the Buddha-nature—the ultimate, eternal and universal principle of which all things are manifestations. In Sanskrit it is called *Tathata* or 'Suchness', a term which has a close affinity with the Chinese *Tao* or the 'Way of things'. This principle is described as the Buddha-nature because to be a Buddha means that one has realized one's identity with *Tathata*, with the one true Self which is not conditioned by distinctions between 'I' and 'You', 'Me' and 'Mine', 'This' and 'That'. It may be natural for us to seek some explanation for man's ignorance of the Buddha-nature, to discover why, if the Self includes all things, man should imagine that it exists only in his own person. This is the old problem: if all things are the One, why does the One become the Many? If there is but one Self, why do men imagine that there are many selves?

To these questions Mahayana Buddhism gives no verbal answer save to point out that questions asked under illusion are themselves part of the illusion. To the awakened consciousness of a Buddha the One has not *become* the Many; it *is* the Many, for as the *Hridaya Sutra* says, 'Form is not different from emptiness (*sunyata*); emptiness is not different from form. Form is precisely emptiness; emptiness is precisely form.' Nor is the ignorant imagination that there are many selves in his eyes a problem demanding an explanation, for the *Vimalakirti Sutra* declares that ignorance and delusive notions (*klesa*) are not different from Enlightenment. An ordinary man is in truth a Buddha just as he is, and if he asks, 'Why, then, don't I know it?' the Mahayana and Zen alike would reply, 'Why do you ask the question?' In other words, this is a way of asking, 'Do you *really* feel that you are a separate self? See if you can experience what you call your ego concretely. Discover the actual sensation which you interpret as your self-hood, and see whether it may not have been misinterpreted. Turn your attention to actual first-hand concrete experience and do not be misled by ideas and conceptions about it.'

Therefore from the very start Zen aimed at clearing aside all definitions, intellectual concepts and speculations; this it did with the most uncompromising thoroughness. It proclaimed at once that both Nirvana and Samsara are the same thing, and that to look for the former outside the latter and to try to reach it by the conventional performance of meritorious deeds is a mere absurdity. Nirvana is here and now, in the midst of Samsara, and there is no question of its being a state of oneness as distinct from a state of many-ness at all; everything depends upon one's own inner realization. A wise man will see Nirvana at once in the ordinary things of life; a fool will philosophize about it and think of it as something else, yet

> An old pine tree preaches wisdom,
> And a wild bird is crying out Truth,

and when master Tung-shan was asked, 'What is the Buddha?' he replied, 'Three pounds of flax.' The whole technique of

The Origins of Zen

Zen was to jolt people out of their intellectual ruts and their conventional morality. The masters asked awkward and unanswerable questions; they made fun of logic and metaphysics; they turned orthodox philosophy upside down in order to make it look absurd. Thus we have master Te-shan saying, 'Nirvana and Bodhi (Enlightenment) are dead stumps to tie your donkey to. The twelve divisions of the scriptures are only lists of ghosts and sheets of paper fit to wipe the dirt from your skin. And all your four merits and ten stages are mere ghosts lingering in their decaying graves. Can these have anything to do with your salvation?'

Zen was first introduced into China by Bodhidharma in A.D. 527. Practically nothing is known of its history in India, and it is probable that Bodhidharma himself only suggested it to the Chinese who evolved it into its present unique form. A story is told that Bodhidharma was brought before the Emperor Wu, who was anxious to see this great sage and to obtain from him some approval of his own devout works. Therefore he asked Bodhidharma:

'We have built temples, copied holy scriptures, ordered monks and nuns to be converted. Is there any merit, Reverend Sir, in our conduct?'

'No merit at all.'

The Emperor, somewhat taken aback, thought that such an answer was upsetting the whole teaching, and inquired again:

'What, then, is the holy truth, the first principle?'

'In vast emptiness there is nothing holy.'

'Who, then, are you to stand before me?'

'I know not, your Majesty.'

Bodhidharma is always depicted by Chinese and Japanese artsists as a fierce old man with a great black beard and large, penetrating eyes. Very little is known about him or his work, and apparently he brought no specific message or teaching to China at all; his influence depended not upon what he did or said, but upon what he *was*, and in neither of his two other recorded interviews with his disciples does he make any statement of his teaching. Shang Kwang (Hui-K'e), his spiritual successor, had to wait standing outside the cave where Bodhidharma was meditating for a whole week before he was admitted. All the time it was snowing, but Shang Kwang was so determined to find out Bodhidharma's secret that he withstood frost-bite and even went to the extreme of cutting off his left arm and presenting it to the master in order to show that he would make any sacrifice for the privilege of being his pupil. At last he was admitted, but Bodhidharma would not give any explanations. All he did was to set him a puzzle which somehow opened his eyes to the truth. Shang Kwang said:

'I have no peace of mind. Might I ask you, Sir, to pacify my mind?'

'Bring out your mind here before me,' replied Bodhidharma. 'I shall pacify it!'

'But it is impossible for me to bring out my mind.'

'Then I have pacified your mind!'

A short time after Bodhidharma's death someone reported that he had seen him among the mountains on the way back to India, walking barefooted and carrying one shoe in his hand. Therefore the master's grave was opened, and all that was found was the single shoe that he had left behind!

For nine years he had remained and nobody knew him;
Carrying a shoe in his hand he went home quietly, without ceremony.

Perhaps it is hard to see anything in such an absurd story as that of Bodhidharma's career which could have altered the whole

32

The Origins of Zen

history of the Far East. An old man comes over from India, is very rude and abrupt with the Emperor, refuses to see a poor wretch who wants some instruction until he has cut off his arm, and then only says something quite unintelligible. Finally he is seen walking about with a shoe in his hand. And yet from that time there began something which inspired artists and writers, soldiers and statesmen, something which has influenced the cultures of China and Japan more than any other single factor. The truth was that Bodhidharma had found wisdom which could only be transmitted to someone prepared to receive it, and then it was a wisdom which could not be put into any intellectual formula. Only those who wanted it so much that, like Shang Kwang, they were prepared to give anything for it could understand. To others it was nonsense, and the absurd legends which have been attached to Bodhidharma probably originated from a desire to emphasize his unconventionality and to give him that slightly humorous atmosphere which always seems to attach itself to the exponents of Zen. Almost all the pictures of Bodhidharma by Zen artists seem to have been calculated to raise a smile.

It is the humorous aspect of Zen which shows one of its important affinities with Taoism, for a similar absence of pompous gravity and seriousness is found in some of the sayings of Lao Tzu and Chuang Tzu. During the years following the death of Bodhidharma and the beginning of Zen as it is known to-day it must undoubtedly have come into close contact with Taoist teachings, for in the sayings of the later masters the word 'Tao' is often used synonymously with 'Buddha-nature' or the 'Dharma' (Law). Perhaps the secret of both Zen and Taoist humour was that neither took the objective world very seriously; they made fun of the cumbersome intellect and of all forms of conventionality and pomposity. When Chuang Tzu's wife died one of his disciples found him singing and beating time on a pot instead of indulging in pious mourning. The disciple remonstrated:

'To live with your wife and then see your eldest son grow up and be a man, and then not to shed a tear over her corpse —this would be bad enough. But to drum on a pot and sing; surely this is going too far.'

'Not at all,' replied the master. 'When she died I could not help being affected by her death. Soon, however, I remembered that she had already existed in a previous state before birth. . . . And now, by virtue of a further change, she is dead, passing from one phase to another like the sequence of spring, summer, autumn and winter. . . . For me to go about weeping and wailing would be to proclaim myself ignorant of these natural laws. Therefore I refrain.'

The particular humour of Zen is found in many of the pictures which the masters have painted of each other. Seldom do we find solemn and dignified personages, but rather lively caricatures of absurdly fat or gnarled little men, roaring with laughter or swearing at some unfortunate disciple who has been unable to find a quick answer for an impossible question. There is one delightful picture of a little bald-headed man leaning on a crooked staff with his tiny eyes sparkling with amusement at two cocks having a scrap in the foreground, while another shows the venerated Sixth Patriarch (Hui Neng), wearing a few shabby rags, engaged in pulling some holy scripture to pieces like a wild maniac. Frequently the Zen masters used to refer to each other as 'old rice-bags' and with other uncomplimentary terms, not out of any professional jealousy, but because it amused them to think that they and their wise and venerated brothers were supposed by ordinary standards to be so especially holy, whereas they had all realized that everything was holy, even cooking-pots and odd leaves blown about by the wind, and that there was nothing particularly venerable about themselves at all. There is another picture by Mu-ch'i showing the master Hsien-tzu chuckling at a shrimp, for whether it is a shrimp or a couple of cocks the Zen masters seemed to find endless wonder and amusement in the most ordinary things. Perhaps their laughter is at the thought that such odd little creatures as these are, just as much as men, embodiments of the sublime Buddha-nature. Or it may also be, to quote Keyserling again, that 'Spirit lacks all gravity and in so far seriousness. Seen from Spirit nothing is heavy; it takes all things lightly. Not only the concept of toil, even that of suffering finds no object in it. There is toil only from the point of view of Gana (the Flesh); and man knows pain and sorrow only as a creature of feeling and emotion. . . . Thus spiritual man must needs impress man of the earth as wanting in seriousness' (*South American Meditations*, p. 373).

But apart from its humour Zen has other connections with Taoism. Lao Tzu, the supposed founder of Taoism, is believed to have been a contemporary of the Buddha (approx. 600 b.c.)[1], and by the time Zen came to China the original philosophy of Lao Tzu had long been overlaid with a wealth of mythology and superstition, for, unlike Confucianism, it had become the religion of the masses. The central concept of

[1] This is the date generally given, although some authorities hold that Lao Tzu is only a mythological character. Mr Arthur Waley gives the date of the *Tao Teh King* (usually ascribed to Lao Tzu) as 240 b.c. and believes that it only became connected with the name of Lao Tzu at a later date. See his *The Way and its Power* (London, 1934), pp. 86, 99 and 101.

35

original Taoism was that of the Tao—a word that has been translated as the Way, the Law, God, Reason, Nature, Meaning and Reality. But actually there is no one English word which can convey its true meaning. The character 'Tao' is composed of symbols signifying rhythm, or periodical movement, and intelligence, but, as Lao Tzu himself says, 'The Tao which can be described in words is not the true Tao' and it is best to leave it untranslated. Suffice it to say that the general idea behind Tao is that of growth and movement; it is the course of nature, the principle governing and causing change, the perpetual movement of life which never for a moment remains still. To Taoism that which is absolutely still or absolutely perfect is absolutely dead, for without the possibility of growth and change there can be no Tao. In reality there is nothing in the universe which is completely perfect or completely still; it is only in the minds of men that such concepts have arisen, and it is just those concepts which, according to Taoism, are at the root of human misery. For man clings on to things in the vain hope that they may remain still and perfect; he does not reconcile himself to the fact of change; he will not let Tao take its course. Thus Lao Tzu and his great exponent, Chuang Tzu, taught that the highest form of man is he who adapts himself to and keeps pace with the movement of Tao. He alone can find peace, for the fact that man notices and regrets change shows that he himself is not moving with the rhythm of life. Movement is only noticeable to something which is relatively still, but this is a false stillness because it creates friction with that which is moving. If man would keep pace with Tao he would find the true stillness, for he would be moving with life and friction would not arise.

This doctrine can very easily degenerate into mere *laissez faire* and thus Taoism eventually became an easy-going

The Origins of Zen

fatalism, whereas the original teaching was nothing of the kind. For coupled with the doctrine of Tao is the teaching of *wu-wei*, the secret of mastering circumstances without asserting oneself against them. *Wu-wei* has been translated by so many Western scholars as non-action and by corrupt Taoism it was held to mean the same thing. Actually it is the principle underlying *ju-jutsu*—a highly successful form of overcoming an opponent in wrestling—the principle of yielding to an on-coming force in such a way that it is unable to harm you, and at the same time changing its direction by pushing it from behind instead of attempting to resist it from the front. Thus the skilled master of life never opposes things; he never tries to change things by asserting himself against them; he yields to their full force and either pushes them slightly out of direct line or else moves them right round in the opposite direction without ever encountering their direct opposition. That is to say, he treats them positively; he changes them by acceptance, by taking them into his confidence, never by flat denial. Perhaps *wu-wei* can best be understood by contrast with its opposite, *yu-wei*. The character for *yu* is composed of two symbols—hand and moon—thus signifying the idea of clutching at the moon as if it could be seized and possessed. But the moon eludes all attempts at grasping, and can never be held still in the sky any more than circumstances can be prevented from changing by conscious striving. Therefore while *yu* is trying to clutch what is elusive (and Life as Tao is essentially elusive), *wu* is not only *not* clutching but also the positive acceptance of elusiveness and change. Thus the highest form of man makes himself a vacuum so that all things are drawn to him; he accepts everything until by including all things he becomes their master. It is the principle of controlling things by going along with them, of mastery through adaptation.

The Spirit of Zen

In a certain sense the concept of Tao is more dynamic than the Mahayana idea of Tathata; the former is something perpetually moving, while the latter is that which is unmoved in the midst of all changes. But the distinction between them is more apparent than real, for only that which accepts change can remain unharmed and truly unmoved. If it is large enough to include all changes it can never itself be changed, and Tathata is the one principle which includes all separate and transitory things. But, as in the case of the Mahayana, the Zen masters saw that to talk about Tao was to miss Tao altogether, for the moment one tries to hold it as a concept it becomes unreal and dead. It is all very well to talk about moving with Tao, but the very fact that one is talking about moving implies that one has not yet begun to move, and the Zen masters were concerned with giving people the initial push. Thus it was Zen that brought Taoism back to life; if for a moment one stops to philosophize and think *about*, life moves on and the living reality of the moment is lost. Therefore the Zen masters had no patience with concepts; conceptual thinking is putting a barrier between oneself and the Tao, and this is absurd for the Tao is here all the time, at every moment ready to be seen but never waiting to be thought about. Thus it is said in the *Mumon-kan*:

> No gate stands on public roads;
> There are paths of various kinds;
> Those who pass this barrier
> Walk freely throughout the universe.

After the death of Bodhidharma there followed him a series of five Zen Patriarchs, of whom the last was Hui Neng. From the time of Hui Neng Zen lost all its distinctively Indian character; it became thoroughly transformed by the

The Origins of Zen

more practical Chinese mentality and whatever traces of intellectual teaching remained were almost entirely swept away. Hui Neng was the last to deliver any distinctly philosophical explanation of Zen, and thereafter most of the few lengthy discourses of Zen masters of which there are records were far more elusive, paradoxical and thoroughgoing. But Hui Neng left a remarkable work—a collection of his sermons written down by one of his disciples—its full title being 'The Sutra Spoken by the Sixth Patriarch on the High Seat of the Gem of Law (Dharmaratha)'. As a rule the term 'sutra' is only applied to the discourses of the Buddha himself or of the great Bodhisattvas who were his immediate disciples, and the one exception to this rule is the 'Sutra of the Sixth Patriarch' which has come to be known as 'the only sutra spoken by a native of China'. This was an honour richly deserved, for this sutra has a place among the *Bhagavad-Gita*, the *Tao Te Ching*, the *Dhammapada* and the *Yoga Sutras* of Patanjali which are universally acknowledged as the greatest masterpieces of Eastern spiritual literature. The first section of the 'Sutra of the Sixth Patriarch' is Hui Neng's account of how he came to an understanding of Zen; in this we are told that he was an illiterate seller of firewood, and that one day while he was working in his shop he overheard someone reciting a passage from the *Diamond Sutra* (*Vajracchedika*) outside in the street. Instantly he obtained an intuitive realization of its meaning, and found that the person reciting the sutra came from the monastery where the Fifth Patriarch, Hung Jan, was instructing a community of some thousand disciples. At once Hui Neng set out in search of the Patriarch, and on coming to the monastery he was set to work in the stables for eight months. One day Hwang Yan, realizing that his time was nearly over, summoned all his disciples and told them that his successor must now be appointed; the privilege was to go to the one who could write the best verse summarizing the teaching of Zen.

At that time the head monk was a certain Shin Hsiu—a man with a thorough intellectual understanding of Buddhism but with no grasp of the essential truth. In his heart he knew that his knowledge was only superficial, and he was afraid to go and submit his verse to the master in person. He decided, therefore, to write it on the wall outside the master's hall, so that if the master should approve he would declare himself to be the author. Thus in the middle of the night he went and wrote this verse:

> The body is like unto the Bodhi-tree,
> And the mind to a mirror bright;
> Carefully we cleanse them hour by hour
> Lest dust should fall upon them.

Publicly the Patriarch expressed his approval of the verse, but in secret he told Shin Hsiu that his understanding was shallow and that before he could allow him to be Sixth Patriarch he must submit another. In the meantime Hui Neng had seen this verse, and realizing that something was wrong he asked a friend to write another by its side, which he would dictate. And this was:

> Neither is there Bodhi-tree,
> Nor yet a mirror bright;
> Since in reality all is void,
> Whereon can the dust fall?

The Patriarch saw at once that here was someone who understood the emptiness of mere conceptions and analogies, and for fear of the jealousy of the other monks, he secretly appointed Hui Neng as his successor, handing over to him the robe and begging-bowl which were supposed to have belonged originally to the Buddha himself. After a series of adventures with jealous pursuers, Hui Neng became recognized as Sixth Patriarch, and his distinctive contribution to Zen was the method of Sudden instead of Gradual realization. The difference was that while some considered it necessary to come to a gradual understanding of Buddhism through patient study and the performance of meritorious deeds, Hui Neng saw that this method easily led one astray into intellectualism. Life is moving too swiftly to be approached tentatively and gradually, for while one makes elaborate preparations for Enlightenment the immediate truth is slipping away all the time. The person who dallies on the edge of the stream, wondering how best to take the plunge, testing the heat of the water with his toes, and thinking about how it will feel when he is in, soon gets into the habit of putting off the issue. The Zen disciple must walk quietly to the edge and slip calmly into the water without further ado, without allowing himself time to conjure up fears and anxious speculations as to what it will be like, or to find elaborate reasons as to why he should not get in at once.

Just before his death Hui Neng announced that the practice of appointing a Patriarch would be discontinued, for he said to his disciples, 'You are all free from doubts, therefore you are all able to carry on the lofty object of our school.' Then he quoted a verse said to have been written by Bodhidharma:

The object of my coming to China
Was to transmit the Teaching of Deliverance to all under delusion.
In five petals the flower will be complete;
Thereafter the fruit will come naturally to maturity.

This was indeed what came to pass, for during the latter part of the T'ang and the whole of the Sung and Yüan dynasties (A.D. 713–1367) which followed on the death of Hui

The Spirit of Zen

Neng the high level attained by the teaching and practice of Zen coincided with the Golden Age of Chinese culture. Almost all the great Zen masters lived in this period—Ma Tsu (Jap. Baso), Po-chang (Jap. Hyakujo), Lin Chi (Jap. Rinzai), Chao-chou (Jap. Joshu) and Yun Men (Jap. Ummon)—many of whom will be quoted in the following chapters. At that time Zen enjoyed a wide popularity among all grades of society, bringing to fruition all that was best in Taoism and the Mahayana. For Zen synthesized the idealism, the immovable serenity and the austerity of Buddhism with the poetry and fluidity of Taoism, with its reverence for the incomplete, the 'imperfect' and the changing as showing the presence of life, of the unending flow of Tao. These two elements pervade the whole spirit of Zen, together with its own unique dynamic quality, which gives life and strength to the other two.

Towards the end of the Sung Dynasty (1279) another form of Buddhism began to arise, and in the following years it gradually diminished the supremacy of Zen in China. This was the cult of Amitabha (Ch. A-mi-to Fo, Jap. Amida), the personification of 'Boundless Light', the great Buddha who had vowed to save all beings and bring them in the end to Nirvana. It was believed that by virtue of this vow all who put their faith in the compassion of Amitabha would be reborn into the Pure Land or Western Paradise (*Sukhavati*)—a place where the attainment of wisdom would be an easier task than in this impossible world. The Western Paradise was described with a wealth of sensuous imagery which very naturally appealed to the masses—

> In that land of true pleasure the flowers never fade,
> Each terraced ascent is of diamond and jade.
> The law of Tathagata sung by each bird
> From thicket and grove in sweet music is heard.

The Origins of Zen

To this day Pure Land Buddhism is the most popular form of the Mahayana in both China and Japan where Amitabha is generally worshipped as a loving God in many ways similar to the God of Christianity. Thus Far Eastern Buddhism was divided into two main schools, known in Japanese as Jiriki and Tariki—'self power' and 'other power'—that is to say, those who relied on their own efforts for the attainment of wisdom and those who relied on the compassion of the Bodhisattvas. Zen belonged to the former, and as the civilization of China began slowly to lose its virility it passed on to the young civilization of Japan, where it was first established by Ei-sai in 1191. Here it became the religion of the samurai—the warrior class—and had an even more profound effect on the culture of the nation than in China; to this day Zen is a powerful factor among the educated Japanese and many professional and business men are in the habit of making periodical visits to Zen monasteries where they live and work with the monks for a few weeks, gathering strength for a return to their ordinary labours. But Zen will go further than Japan. Already a hostel for Western students has been attached to a monastery at Kyoto, and whether under the name of Zen or not, something of its spirit must enter wherever religions and philosophies are to be roused from the grave of theories and words.

The Secret of Zen

A Confucian poet once came to Zen master Hui-t'ang to inquire the secret of his teaching, whereupon the master quoted to him one of the sayings of Confucius: 'Do you think I am hiding things from you, O my disciples? Indeed, I have nothing to hide from you.' Since Hui-t'ang would not allow him to ask any more questions, the poet went away deeply puzzled, but a short time after the two went for a walk together in the mountains. As they were passing a bush of wild laurel the master turned to his companion and asked, 'Do you smell it?' Then to the answer, 'Yes,' he remarked, 'There, I have nothing to hide from you!' At once the poet was enlightened.[1] For it is really a paradox to speak of the secret of Zen, and in spite of all the apparently abstruse or ridiculous answers of the Zen masters to the urgent questionings of their disciples, nothing is being hidden from us. The truth is that Zen is so hard to understand, just because it is so obvious, and we miss it time and time again because we are looking for something obscure; with our eyes on the horizon we do not see what lies at our feet. In the words of Hakuin's 'Song of Meditation':

> All beings are from the very beginning the Buddhas;
> It is like ice and water:
> Apart from water no ice can exist.
> Outside sentient beings, where do we seek the Buddha?

[1] This and most of the other Zen stories (*mondo*) quoted have been translated by Professor Suzuki, and large numbers of them will be found in his various works.

The Secret of Zen

Not knowing how near Truth is,
People seek it far away. . . .
They are like him who, in the midst of water,
Cries out in thirst so imploringly.

(*Trans.* SUZUKI.)

Man is often too proud to examine the self-evident things which are closest to him. Zen found the followers of the Mahayana looking for truth to scriptures, to holy men and Buddhas, believing that they would reveal it to them if they lived the good life. For man's apparent humility in thinking that wisdom is something too sublime to reveal itself in the ordinary affairs of his life is a subtle form of pride. Inwardly he feels that he must be so great as to be removed from the things of the world before he can receive truth, and such is his pride that he will only deign to receive it from the lips of sages and from the pages of sacred scriptures. He does not see it in human beings or in the incidents of everyday life; he does not see it in himself, for again he is too proud to see himself as he is. So far from seeking for truth he hides his imperfections under his 'meritorious deeds' and approaches the Buddhas from behind their mask.

To Zen this careful self-preparation for finding the truth at some future time or from some external source is putting off the issue of seeing the facts just as they are at the moment, be they good or evil. For to him who cannot see the truth in himself no Buddha can reveal it, and he who does not look for it this moment cannot expect to be shown it in the future. And so Zen taught that nobody could find the Buddha in a Paradise or in any celestial realm until he had first found it in himself and in other sentient beings, and nobody could expect to find enlightenment in a hermitage unless he was capable of finding it in the life of the world. For the first

The Spirit of Zen

principle of the Mahayana is that all things, however vile on the surface and however insignificant, are aspects of the Buddha-nature, and this implies that every being and thing must be accepted; nothing can be excluded from the 'Lotus Land of Purity' as being 'worldly' or 'trivial' or 'base'. As Thomas à Kempis wrote in the *Imitation of Christ*, 'If thy heart were right, then every creature would be a mirror of life and a book of holy doctrine. There is no creature so small and abject, but it reflects the goodness of God,' and to the question 'What is Enlightenment?' a Zen master replied, 'Your everyday thoughts,' while another when asked, 'What is the Tao?' answered, 'Usual life is the very Tao.' Master Po-chang said that Zen meant simply, 'Eat when you are hungry, sleep when you are tired,' while Lin-chi declared that 'the truly religious man has nothing to do but go on with his life as he finds it in the various circumstances of this worldly existence. He rises quietly in the morning, puts on his clothes and goes out to work. When he wants to walk, he walks; when he wants to sit, he sits. He has no hankering after Buddhahood, not the remotest thought of it. How is this possible? A wise man of old says, If you strive after Buddhahood by any conscious contrivances, your Buddha is indeed the source of eternal transmigration' (Suzuki, *Essays in Zen Buddhism*, II, p. 260).

If all things are in reality the Tao or the Buddha-nature, what is the use of striving to become a Buddha and to attain Nirvana? For those who have eyes to see, eternal truth and Buddhahood are manifested plainly before us here and now, in our own thoughts and actions, and in the changing stream of events which is flowing past us all the time. Hence there is no object in seeking after Buddhahood as if it were something other than life as it is; in the words of Hui Neng, 'The

only difference between a Buddha and an ordinary man is
that one realizes it while the other does not.'

> This very earth is the Lotus Land of Purity,
> And this body is the body of Buddha.
>
> (HAKUIN.)

Therefore Zen interprets striving after Buddhahood as imply-
ing a distinction between oneself and the Buddha-nature;
that is the foundation of egoism, for it means that the self
has been separated from the rest of life, that it has become
isolated from other beings, and this is a lesser form of lunacy,
for the lunatic is the most isolated person in the world. Therefore all external ideas of the Buddha and Nirvana were
uncompromisingly swept aside, and Zen became a form of
iconoclasm. It ruthlessly broke down all conceptions and
symbols, all external and anthropomorphic ideas of the
Buddha, which masqueraded as the truth. Thus we have
Lin-chi declaiming:

> O you followers of Truth! If you wish to obtain an orthodox
> understanding of Zen, do not be deceived by others. Inwardly or
> outwardly, if you encounter any obstacles kill them right away.
> If you encounter the Buddha, kill him; if you encounter the
> Patriarch, kill him; . . . kill them all without hesitation, for this is
> the only way to deliverance. Do not get yourselves entangled
> with any object, but stand above, pass on, and be free!
>
> (*Trans.* SUZUKI.)

Again there is the Zen saying, 'Do not linger about where
the Buddha is, and as to where he is not, pass swiftly on.' An
amusing story in this connection is that of master Tan-hsia
and the wooden Buddha. One winter night Tan-hsia took
shelter in a temple, and finding that the fire was going out he
took down one of the wooden figures of the Buddha from

the altar and placed it on the embers. When the keeper of the temple discovered what had been done he was furious at such an act of sacrilege and began to scold Tan-hsia for his irreverence. But Tan-hsia merely scratched about among the ashes, remarking, 'I am gathering the holy relics from the burnt ashes.'

'How,' asked the keeper, 'can you get holy relics from a wooden Buddha?'

'If there are no holy relics,' replied Tan-hsia, 'this is certainly not a Buddha and I am committing no sacrilege. May I have the two remaining Buddhas for my fire?'

Zen was therefore the direct method of approach; it dispensed with external aids to religion as liable to lead people into confusion. Scriptures and doctrines were well so long as they were seen only as aids, and Zen masters likened them to a finger pointing at the moon; he is a fool who takes the finger for the moon. Thus Zen has been summed up as:

> A special transmission outside the Scriptures;
> No dependence upon words and letters;
> Direct pointing to the mind of man;
> Seeing into one's own nature.

But while we may be told that the truth of Zen is obvious, that it is standing before our eyes every moment of the day, this does not take us very far. There seems to be nothing remarkable about the ordinary affairs of life; there appears to be nothing in putting on one's clothes, eating one's food or washing one's hands which would indicate the presence of Nirvana and Buddhahood. Yet when a monk asked master Nan-ch'uan, 'What is the Tao?' he replied, 'Usual life is the very Tao.' The monk asked again, 'How can we accord with it?' (i.e. 'How can we bring ourselves into harmony and unity with it?'). Nan-ch'uan answered, 'If you try to accord with it, you will get away from it.' For life, even as the ordinary humdrum series of daily events, is something essentially ungraspable and indefinable; never for a moment does it remain the same; we can never make it stand still for analysis and definition. If we try to think of the speed at which time is passing or at which things are changing our minds are set in a whirl, for it is a speed which can never be calculated. The harder we try to catch hold of the moment, to seize a pleasant sensation, or to define something in a way which will be satisfactory for all time, the more elusive it becomes. It has been said that to define is to kill, and if the wind were to stop for one second for us to catch hold of it, it would cease to be wind. The same is true of life. Perpetually things and events are moving and changing; we cannot take hold of the present moment and make it stay with us; we cannot call back past time or keep for ever a passing sensation. Once we try to do this all we have is a dead memory; the reality is not there, and no satisfaction can be found in it. If we suddenly realize that we are happy, the more we endeavour to think of some means of preserving our happiness, the faster we see it slipping away. We try to define happiness so that we may know how to find it when we are feeling miserable; a man thinks, 'I am happy now that I am staying in this place. Therefore happiness, for me, is to come and stay in this place.' And the next time he is unhappy he tries to apply this definition; he goes to that place again and finds that it does not make him happy; there is only the dead memory of happiness, and the definition does not hold. For happiness is like Maeterlinck's blue birds —try to capture them and they lose their colour; it is like trying to clutch water in one's hands—the harder one grips, the faster it slips through one's fingers. Therefore a Zen master when asked, 'What is the Tao?' replied immediately, 'Walk on!' for we can only understand life by keeping pace with it, by a complete affirmation and acceptance of its magic-like transformations and unending changes. By this accept-ance the Zen disciple is filled with a great sense of wonder, for everything is perpetually becoming new. The beginning of the universe is now, for all things are at this moment being created, and the end of the universe is now, for all things are at this moment passing away. Therefore the Zen poet P'ang-yün says:

> How wondrously supernatural,
> And how miraculous this!
> I draw water, and I carry fuel!
> (*Trans.* SUZUKI.)

Thus Zen is sometimes described as 'straightforwardness' or 'going right ahead', for Zen is to move with life without trying to arrest and interrupt its flow; it is an immediate awareness of things as they live and move, as distinct from the mere grasp of ideas and feelings *about* things which are the dead symbols of a living reality. Therefore master Takuan says in relation to the art of fencing (*kendo*)—an art strongly influenced by the principles of Zen—

> This—what may be termed the 'non-interfering' attitude of mind—constitutes the most vital element in the art of fencing as well as in Zen. If there is any room left even for the breadth of a hair between two actions, this is interruption.

That is to say, the contact between an event and the mind's response thereto should not be broken by discursive thinking, for, he continues,

> When the hands are clapped, the sound issues without a

moment's deliberation. The sound does not wait and think before it issues. There is no mediacy here; one movement follows another without being interrupted by one's conscious mind. If you are troubled and cogitate what to do, seeing the opponent about to strike you down, you give him room, that is, a happy chance for his deadly blow. Let your defence follow the attack without a moment's interruption, and there will be no two separate movements to be known as attack and defence.

Hence if 'attack' represents the external world, or life, and 'defence' one's response to life, this must be taken to mean that the distinction between 'self' and 'life' is destroyed; egoism disappears when the contact between the two is so immediate that they move together, keeping in the same rhythm. Takuan says further:

> This immediateness of action on your part will inevitably end in the opponent's self-defeat. It is like a boat smoothly gliding down the rapids; in Zen, and in fencing as well, a mind of no-hesitation, no-interruption, no-mediacy, is highly valued. So much reference is made in Zen to a flash of lightning or to sparks issuing from the impact of two flint-stones. If this is understood in the sense of quickness, a grievous mistake is committed. The idea is to show immediateness of action, an uninterrupted movement of life-energy. Whenever room is left for interruption from a quarter not at all in vital relation with the occasion, you are sure to lose your own position. This of course does not mean to desire to do things rashly or in the quickest possible time. If there were this desire in you its very presence would be an interruption.
>
> (*Trans.* SUZUKI.)[1]

This is in many ways similar to the art of listening to music;

[1] The above translation of Takuan's advice is taken from Vol. III of Professor Suzuki's *Essays in Zen Buddhism*, p. 319. See also the section on Judo and Kendo, p. 106.

if one stops to consider one's emotional or intellectual reactions to a symphony while it is being played, to analyse the construction of a chord, or to linger over a particular phrase, the melody is lost. To hear the whole symphony one must concentrate on the flow of notes and harmonies as they come into being and pass away, keeping one's mind continuously in the same rhythm. To think over what has passed, to wonder what is about to come, or to analyse the effect upon oneself is to interrupt the symphony and to lose the reality. The whole attention must be directed to the symphony and oneself must be forgotten; if any conscious attempt is made to concentrate upon the symphony, the mind is led away by the thought of oneself trying to concentrate, and it was for this reason that Nan-ch'uan told the monk that if he *tried* to accord with the Tao he would get away from it. Therefore Zen went further than telling man to listen to the symphony instead of thinking about his reactions to it, for even to tell someone not to think about his independent reactions is to make him think about not thinking about them! Therefore Zen adopted the positive method of emphasizing the symphony of life itself; all talk about trying to bring the mind into harmony introduces the concept of the self which is trying, thereby drawing the attention away from the actual fact of life. It was this to which the Zen masters pointed; they simply demonstrated life without making any assertions or denials *about* it. Therefore one would say to his disciple, 'Beyond assertion and denial show me the truth of Zen. Quick, quick, or thirty blows for you!' The disciple had no time to stop and think out an answer; the master expected it to come as immediately and as spontaneously as life itself is moving. A master once held up a stick before a gathering of his disciples and said, 'O monks, do you see this? If you see it, what is it you see? Would you say, "It is a stick"? If you do you are ordinary people, you have no Zen. But if you say, "We do not see any stick," then I would say: Here I hold one, and how can you deny the fact?' The particular stick in question was known as the *shippe*, the master's symbol of office, and it was often used to demonstrate Zen since it always lay close to the master's hand. Master Hsiang-yen once asked a disciple:

'There was once a monk who asked Wei-shan why Bodhidharma had come to China, and Wei-shan in answer held up his *shippe*. Now how do you understand the meaning of Wei-shan's action?'

'The master's idea,' replied the disciple, 'is to elucidate mind along with matter, to reveal truth by means of an objective reality.'

'Your understanding,' said the master, 'is all right as far as it goes. But what is the use of hurrying so to theorize?'

Whereupon the disciple asked, 'What, then, will be your understanding?'

Hsiang-yen held up his *shippe*.

Master Po-chang once set a pitcher before two of his disciples, saying, 'Do not call it a pitcher, but tell me what it is.'

One of them answered, 'It cannot be called a piece of wood.'

But Po-chang considered this answer beside the point, whereupon he asked the other the same question, and in reply he came forward, pushed the pitcher over and walked away. As a result Po-chang appointed this disciple as his successor.

It was in this way that the Zen masters brought the minds of their disciples into direct contact with life, with the constantly changing and moving process which is the Buddha-nature perpetually manifesting itself. To know the Buddha-nature was to know life apart from 'interruptions', the chief of which was the concept of the self as an entity distinct from life, occupied entirely with its own private reactions to reality as distinct from reality itself. The Buddha had taught that the cause of this folly was *Trishna* (Pali *Tanha*), which is so often mistranslated as 'Desire'. Literally it means 'Thirst', and from this it came to mean 'thirst for life', while in the context of the Buddha's teaching it undoubtedly meant thirst for life as an isolated being, as one who stands outside and considers primarily the effect which life is having and will have upon himself. Apart from this effect he has no realization of life whatever, and thus he never actually lives; to return to the analogy of music, he is like one who is so occupied with his own feelings about a tune that the tune is only half heard, for while he is thinking over the effects of the first bar the orchestra has played several more which he misses altogether. But while the philosophers of the Mahayana were considering these things intellectually, being concerned with the ideas rather than the realities, Zen passed beyond all discursive thinking. When asked about the ultimate mysteries of Buddhism, it replied, 'The cypress tree in the courtyard!' 'The bamboo grove at the foot of the hill!' 'The dried up dirt scraper!' Anything to bring the mind back from abstractions to life!

Closely connected with the foregoing is another important aspect of Zen, which may be called 'spiritual poverty'. Almost every form of religion has insisted that many possessions are a bar to spiritual progress, but while the Zen monk has certainly the minimum of material possessions, Zen interprets poverty as an attitude of mind rather than a physical condition. One of the most common ways of trying to fix life into rigid definitions is to qualify something, whether a person, a thing or an idea, with the statement, 'This belongs to me.' But because life is this elusive and perpetually changing process, every time we think we have really taken possession of something, the truth is that we have completely lost it. All that we possess is our own idea about the thing desired—an idea which tends to remain fixed, which does not grow as the thing grows. Thus one of the most noticeable facts about those obsessed with greed for possessions, whether material goods or cherished ideas, is their desire that things shall remain as they are—not only that their possessions shall remain in their own hands, but also that the possessions themselves shall not change. There are theologians and philosophers who show the greatest concern if anyone questions their ideas about the universe, for they imagine that within those ideas they have at last enshrined ultimate truth, and that to lose those ideas would be to lose the truth. But because truth is alive it will not be bound by anything which shows no sign of life— namely, a conception whose validity is held to depend partly on the fact that it is unchangeable. For once we imagine that we have grasped the truth of life, the truth has vanished, for truth cannot become anyone's property, the reason being that truth *is* life, and for one person to think that he posssesses all life is a manifest absurdity. The part cannot possess the whole. Therefore Chuang-Tzu tells the following story:

Shun asked Ch'eng, saying, 'Can one get Tao so as to have it for one's own?'

'Your very body,' replied Ch'eng, 'is not your own. How should Tao be?'

'If my body,' said Shun, 'is not my own, pray whose is it?'

'It is the delegated image of Tao,' replied Ch'eng. 'Your life is not your own. It is the delegated harmony of Tao. Your individuality is not your own. It is the delegated adaptability of Tao.

... You move, but know not how. You are at rest, but know not why. ... These are the operation of the laws of Tao. How then should you get Tao so as to have it for your own?'

Just as no person can possess life, so no idea which a person may possess can define it; the idea of possession is illusory, for apart from the fact that all things must eventually pass away into some other form, and can never remain in one place for eternity, at the root of possession lies the desire that things shall not alter in any way, and this is a complete impossibility. If, therefore, life can never be grasped, how can it ever be understood? How can truth be known if it can never be defined? Zen would answer: by not trying to grasp or define it, and this is the fundamental Buddhist ideal of non-attachment, or the Taoist ideal of *wu-wei*.

But Buddhism and Taoism go further than saying that nothing can ever be possessed; they declare that those who try to possess are in fact *possessed*, they are slaves to their own illusions about life. Spiritual freedom is just that capacity to be as spontaneous and unfettered as life itself, to be 'as the wind that bloweth where it listeth and thou hearest the sound thereof but cannot tell whence it cometh nor whither it goeth.' 'Even so,' said Jesus, 'is everyone that is born of the Spirit.' But non-attachment does not mean running away from things to some peaceful hermitage, for we can never escape from our own illusions about life; we carry them with us, and if we are afraid of them and wish to escape it means that we are doubly enslaved. For whether we are content with our illusions or frightened of them, we are equally possessed by them, and hence the non-attachment of Buddhism and Taoism means not running away from life but running with it, for freedom comes through complete acceptance of reality. Those who wish to keep their illusions do not move at all; those who fear them run backwards into greater illusions, while those who conquer them 'Walk on'.

Thus the poverty of the Zen disciple is the negative aspect of his spiritual freedom; he is poor in the sense that his mind is not encumbered with material and intellectual *impedimenta*— the significant Latin word for 'baggage'. This state of mind is the realization of the Mahayana doctrine of *sunyata*, of the emptiness of all transitory things; nothing can be grasped, for everything is emptiness; nor is there anything which can grasp, for the self is emptiness. Therefore the *Yuen-Chioh Sutra* declares that all component things are 'like drifting clouds, like the waning moon, like ships that sail the ocean, like shores that are washed away', and the Zen masters, realizing the evanescence of the outer world, of their own ideas and of the ego itself, cease to cling to these passing forms. In the words of the *Dhammapada* they are 'those who have no possessions . . . who have realized the causeless and unconditioned freedom through understanding the emptiness of that which passes away—the track of these men it is impossible to trace just as the track of birds in the sky cannot be followed.' For the Zen life does not move in ruts; it is the freedom of the Spirit, unfettered by external circumstances and internal illusions. Its very nature is such that it cannot be described in words, and the nearest we can get to it is by analogy. It is like the wind moving across the face of the earth, never stopping at any particular place, never attaching itself to any particular object, always adapting itself to the rise and fall of the ground. If such analogies give the impression of a dreamy *laissez faire*, it must be remembered that Zen is not always a gentle breeze, like decadent Taoism; more than often it is a fierce gale which sweeps everything ruthlessly before it, an icy blast which penetrates to the heart of everything and passes right through to the other side! The freedom and poverty of Zen is to leave everything and 'Walk on', for this is what life itself does, and Zen is the religion of life.

Therefore the masters tell their disciples to forget all that they have ever learnt before coming to the practice of Zen, to forget even their knowledge of Buddhism. For the Buddha himself declared that his teaching was only a raft with which to cross a river; when the opposite bank has been reached it must be left behind, but so many of his followers mistook the raft for the opposite bank. Yet this negative aspect of Zen, this giving up, is only another way of expressing the positive fact that to give up everything is to gain all. 'He that loseth his life shall find it.' Professor Suzuki points out that while it was the custom of some of the masters to express their poverty, others would refer rather to the complete sufficiency of things. Thus while Hsiang-yen says:

> My last year's poverty was not poverty enough;
> My poverty this year is poverty indeed.
> In my poverty last year there was room for a gimlet's point;
> But this year even the gimlet has gone—

Mumon emphasizes the other side of the picture:

> Hundreds of spring flowers, the autumnal moon,
> A refreshing summer breeze, winter snow—
> Free thy mind from idle thoughts,
> And for thee how enjoyable every season is!

Here we find the acceptance and affirmation of the seasonal changes, and in the same way Zen accepts and affirms the birth, growth, decay and death of men; there are no regrets for the past, and no fears for the future. Thus the Zen disciple gains all by accepting all, since ordinary possessiveness is loss

—it is the denial of the right of people and things to live and change; hence the only loss in Zen is the loss of this denial.

After all this the Western student will naturally be wondering where ordinary morality comes into Zen. Every religion has had its moral code, and the Buddha summed up his teaching in the words:

> Cease to do evil;
> Learn to do well;
> Cleanse your own heart—
> This is the way of the Buddhas.

It will be asked if there is not a grave danger in the Zen practice of accepting all things, both good and evil, as manifestations of the Buddha-nature, for on such grounds it might be possible to justify any form of action. Indeed, this is a difficulty with which the Zen masters have had to reckon; immature disciples would frequently make the all-inclusiveness of Zen an excuse for pure libertinism, and it is for this reason that the members of Zen communities observe a rigid discipline. The solution to the difficulty is that no one should undertake the practice of Zen without first having adapted himself to a thorough moral discipline. While morality should not be confused with religion, it does take one a certain distance towards the goal; it cannot go the whole way because it is essentially rigid, intellectual and limiting, and Zen begins where morality leaves off. At the same time, morality is valuable so long as it is recognized as a means to an end; it is a good servant, but a terrible master. When men use it as a servant it enables them to adapt themselves to society, to mix easily with their fellows, and most especially it permits freedom for spiritual development. When it is their master, they become bigots and conventional ethical machines. But as a means to an end it makes social existence possible; it guarantees men against obstruction from their fellows, and while it does not of itself produce spiritual understanding, it provides the necessary freedom for spiritual development. A garden has to be disciplined so that the plants and flowers do not strangle each other, but the beauty of the garden is not in the discipline so much as in the things whose growth it has made possible. And just as the garden must be cultivated and planned before the flowers are allowed to grow, so the moral law must be mastered before the spiritual law, for just as the flowers might strangle each other, so might the followers of the spirit become wild libertines. Yet morality, in the ethical sense of being adapted to society, is not by itself sufficient preparation for Zen. Something stronger than this is needed if the tremendous power of the spirit is to be born in man without running amok, and that is self-discipline. In the fullest sense of the term this virtue is rare in human society, although no society can exist for long without it, and the long duration of Chinese civilization as compared with that of ancient Greece must primarily be attributed to the insistence of both Confucianism and Buddhism on a rigid self-discipline.

Therefore the Zen masters have always insisted on a severe training as a preliminary to the practice of Zen. This training is picturesquely referred to as 'the long maturing of the sacred womb', and numerous stories are told of the discipline which the masters imposed upon themselves in the early stages of their development, of how they brought their thoughts and emotions under complete control, how they hardened themselves to frost and snow in broken-down temples where 'there were no roofs and the stars shone through at night'. There is a remarkable series of pictures known as the 'Ten Stages of Spiritual Cow-herding' which demonstrate this point

The Secret of Zen

particularly well. The task of understanding Zen is repre-
sented under the allegory of a man catching and herding a cow,
which is intended to symbolize the mind. There are ten pictures, showing the cow being traced, caught and brought
under control until it is sufficiently well-behaved for the man
to ride home on its back. Then the cow is forgotten, and the
man is seen sitting quietly in his hut, while the next picture is
just a blank circle entitled, 'The Cow and the Man both gone
out of sight', for all illusions have been conquered and the
whole objective world is seen as emptiness. But this is not all,
for though the disciple has realized the evanescence of all forms
he has not yet made direct contact with life itself; he has seen
things as such as illusions, but he has not realized their fundamental Buddha-nature. Therefore the next picture is called
'Back to the Origin, back to the Source' and shows just a few
sprays of grass by a stream, while in the last picture we see the
Bodhisattva communicating what he has found to others in
the form of the rotund, jolly Pu Tai—the god of good for-
tune, who 'enters the city with bliss-bestowing hands'. In
the fifth picture where the cow is being led carefully back to
the path the verse attached to it reads:

> Never let yourself be separated
> From the whip and the tether,
> Lest she should wander away
> Into a world of defilement;
> When she is properly tended
> She will grow pure and docile;
> Even without chain, nothing binding,
> She will by herself follow you.

Restrictions can be discarded when the mind has been thoroughly controlled and made to adopt right habits, but it is not
until the last picture of all that the man 'goes on his own way

63

without following the steps of the ancient sages. Carrying a gourd he goes out into the market; leaning against a stick he comes home. He is found in company with wine-bibbers and butchers; he and they are all converted into Buddhas.'[1]

[1] The Cowherding Pictures, complete with the commentaries and verses attached to them, will be found at the end of the first volume of Professor Suzuki's *Essays in Zen Buddhism*. Two other versions of these pictures will be found in his *Manual of Zen Buddhism*.

The Technique of Zen

Described in words, Zen has much in common with many other religions and philosophies; the ideas of poverty, freedom, acceptance and direct contact with reality set forward in the previous chapter are found also in Taoism, Vedanta, Sufiism and the writings of many Christian mystics. Though Zen may go somewhat further than other systems in all these things, it is in no way radically different so far as the ultimate spiritual experience is concerned. In its methods, however, it is unique. Whereas the fate of almost every cult is to fall away in time from the spirit of its early followers, Zen has been able to preserve that spirit up to the present day; after more than 1,400 years it has in no way degenerated into mere 'philosophism' or into the formal observance of precepts of which the original meaning is no longer known. There are two reasons for this; firstly, that the criterion of Zen is a spiritual experience so definite that there can be no mistaking it, and secondly, that the early masters devised a means of passing on their teaching which can never be explained away by the intellect—a means which, if put into use at all, can only have one result, and that is this spiritual experience. These two factors are inseparable; the first is known as *Satori* and the second as the *Koan* (pron. *Ko-an*).

Satori is a definite experience in so far as the manner of its coming and its effects upon character are concerned; otherwise it is indefinable, for it is the sudden realization of the truth of Zen. Essentially Satori is a sudden experience, and it is often described as a 'turning over' of the mind, just as a pair of

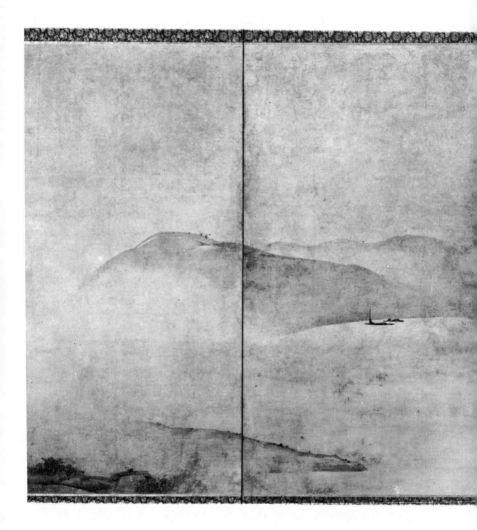

scales will suddenly turn over when a sufficient amount of material has been poured into one pan to overbalance the weight in the other. Hence it is an experience which generally occurs after a long and concentrated effort to discover the meaning of Zen. Its immediate cause may be the most trivial event, while its effect has been described by Zen masters in the most astonishing terms. A master wrote of his own experience, 'It was beyond description and altogether incommunicable, for there was nothing in the world to which it could be compared. . . . As I looked round and up and down, the whole universe with its multitudinous sense-objects now appeared quite different; what was loathsome before, together with ignorance and passions, was seen to be nothing else but the outflow of my own inmost nature, which in itself remained bright, true and transparent.' Another wrote, 'Whatever doubts and indecisions I had before were completely dissolved like a piece of thawing ice. I called out loudly, "How wondrous! How wondrous! There is no birth-and-death from which one has to escape, nor is there any supreme knowledge after which one has to strive." '

Some descriptions are even more vivid than these; in many cases it seemed as though the bottom had fallen out of the universe, as though the oppressiveness of the outer world had suddenly melted like a vast mountain of ice, for Satori is release from one's habitual state of tenseness, of clinging to false ideas of possession. The whole rigid structure which is man's usual interpretation of life suddenly drops to pieces, resulting in a sense of boundless freedom, and the test of true Satori is that he who experiences it has not the slightest doubt as to the completeness of his release. If there is anywhere the least uncertainty, the least feeling of 'this is too good to be true', then the Satori is only partial, for it implies the desire to cling to the experience lest it should be lost, and until that desire is overcome the experience can never be complete. The wish to hold fast to Satori, to make sure that one possesses it, kills it in just the same way as it kills every other experience. But one's own feeling of certainty is not the only test of Satori; the experienced master can tell at once whether the disciple has any doubts, firstly, by his intuition, and secondly, by testing the disciple with a Koan.

While Satori is 'the measure of Zen', because without it there can be no Zen at all, only a heap of nonsense, the Koan is the measure of Satori. Literally the word 'Koan' means 'a public document', but it has come to mean a form of problem based on the actions and sayings of famous masters. It is a problem which admits of no intellectual solution; the answer has no *logical* connection with the question, and the question is of such a kind as to baffle the intellect altogether. Here are some examples:

'A sound is made by the clapping of two hands. What is the sound of one hand?'

'A long time ago a man kept a goose in a bottle. It grew larger and larger until it could not get out of the bottle any more; he did not want to break the bottle, nor did he wish to hurt the goose; how would you get it out?'

'When the Many are reduced to the One, to what is the One to be reduced?'

'Here is a man on a tree holding one of the branches in his mouth, but neither clinging to any of them with his hands nor touching the trunk with his feet. Someone at the foot of the tree asks him, "What is Zen?" If he does not answer the question, he cannot satisfy the man, but if he speaks, even a word, he will at once fall down to death. At such a moment, what answer would you make if you were he?'

To Westerners these Koans may appear as pure rubbish, reminiscent of 'Why is a mouse when it spins?' But it will be noticed that all of these Koans involve one in some kind of dilemma; there is generally a choice between two alternatives, both of which are equally impossible. Thus each Koan reflects the giant Koan of life, for to Zen the problem of life is to pass beyond the two alternatives of assertion and denial, both of which obscure the truth. Thus a less 'nonsensical' Koan is the already quoted, 'Beyond assertion and denial say one word of Zen, or thirty blows for you!' Every Koan must eventually lead to this impasse. One begins by trying to grapple with it intellectually; it is found to contain a certain amount of symbolism and analogy. Thus in the tale about the goose we find that the goose represents man and the bottle his circumstances; he must either abandon the world so as to be free of it, or else be crushed by it, but both of these alternatives are forms of suicide. What purpose is to be served by abandoning the world, and what can we achieve if we allow it to crush us? Here is the fundamental dilemma with which the Zen disciple is confronted, and somehow he must find a way through. The moment he finds it there comes the flash of Satori; the goose is out of the bottle and the bottle is unbroken, for suddenly the disciple has escaped from the bondage of his own imaginary prison—the rigid view of life which he himself has created out of his desire for possession. Thus to the question, 'How shall I escape from the Wheel of Birth and Death?' a master replied, 'Who puts you under restraint?'

Many Western students are under the impression that Zen 'meditation' (i.e. work on the Koan) is a form of self-hypnosis, its object being to induce a state of trance. Acting on this impression, Mr Arthur Waley has described Zen as 'Quietism', Reischauer as 'mystical self-intoxication', and Griffiths as 'mind murder and the curse of idle reverie' (*Religions of Japan*, p. 255). The exact opposite is the truth; work with a Koan, to be successful, must have none of the passivity of Quietism; as for 'mind murder and the curse of idle reverie', a few days' sojourn in a Zen community would dispose of any suspicion of idle reverie, while the accusation that Zen is 'mind murder' is no more true than the charge that it upsets all morality. For like morality, the mind (intellect) is a good servant and a bad master, and while the rule is for men to become enslaved by their intellectual modes of thought, Zen aims at controlling and surpassing the intellect, but as in the case of the goose and the bottle, the intellect, like the bottle, is not destroyed. For the Koan is not a means of inducing trance as if some kind of trance were the highest possible attainment for human beings; it is simply a means of breaking through a barrier, or as the Zen masters describe it, it is a brick with which to knock at a door; when the door is opened, the brick may be thrown away, and this door is the rigid barrier which man erects between himself and spiritual freedom. When the door is opened at the moment of Satori, the disciple passes not into a trance but into a new attitude towards life which reflects itself in a character of remarkable beauty. These misinformed Western critics must be confusing Zen proper with a schism certainly as old as the time of Hui Neng, the Sixth Patriarch, who remarked that there were some disciples who imagined that all one had to do was to sit still with a perfectly vacant mind, but on more than one occasion he said emphatically that such persons were no better than inanimate objects, than blocks of wood and pieces of stone.

The Spirit of Zen

Far from being an exercise in passivity, the Koan involves the most tremendous mental and spiritual struggle, requiring what the masters call a 'great spirit of inquiry'. Thus master Ku-mei Yu writes: 'Once lifted up before the mind, never let the Koan slip off; try to see with all the persistence you find in yourself into the meaning of the Koan given you, and never once waver in your determination to get into the very bottom of the matter. . . . Do not make a guess-work of your Koan; do not search for its meaning in the literature you have learned; go straight at it without leaning on any kind of intermediary help.' Once work upon a Koan has been started a whole mass of ideas will arise in the mind—symbolical meanings, associations, possible solutions and all manner of wandering thoughts. These must be ruthlessly thrust aside, and the more insistent they become, the more intensely must the disciple concentrate on the Koan itself, striving to penetrate the dilemma which it presents. From time to time the master will interview the disciple to find out how he is progressing, and as often as the disciple offers a merely intellectual and logically thought out solution the master will disapprove and tell him to try again. Usually this process will continue for several years, until the disciple eventually reaches a complete impasse; he realizes that every intellectual solution is futile; he arrives at a state where the dilemma of life enshrined in the Koan becomes an overpowering reality and a problem so urgent that it has been compared to a ball of red-hot iron stuck in one's throat. Philosophically, we may understand perfectly that the great problem of life is to get the goose out of the bottle without hurting either, to pass beyond assertion and negation, to find release from the impossible alternatives of overcoming the world by attempting to possess everything, or of letting ourselves be completely ruled by circumstances.

The Technique of Zen

But that does not mean that we realize the problem as the most urgent of all necessities. The choice is between asserting ourselves against the world, trying to make all things submit to us, and, on the other hand, giving way entirely to 'Fate', denying our own capacity to achieve anything. Most of us shun the latter and attempt feebly to realize the former, by clinging fast to our mental and physical possessions, hoping gradually to add to their store. And while this first alternative can never possibly be achieved, since the more we grasp the faster do the objects of our desire slip away, the thought of the second fills us with the horror of eternal death. If this ever occurs to us as a problem it is only in a remote and philosophical way; it seems as far off as the Day of Judgement, and since there is plenty of time between now and then we can hope for a possible solution to 'turn up'.

But work with a Koan makes the problem an immediate reality, and when the impasse is reached the disciple is likened to a pursued rat that has run up a blind tunnel, to a man who has climbed to the end of a pole or reached the edge of a precipice in an attempt to flee from a raging fire. It is just when this most hopeless stage has been reached that the masters urge their disciples to redouble their efforts. A way must be found off the end of the pole and the rat must gather all its strength to break through the tunnel walls. In a work called *The Mirror for Zen Students* compiled by the master T'ui-yin it is said, 'As the inquiry goes on steadily and uninterruptedly you will come to see that there is no intellectual clue in the Koan, that it is altogether devoid of sense as you ordinarily understand the word, that it is entirely flat, devoid of taste, has nothing appetizing about it, and that you are beginning to have a certain feeling of uneasiness and impatience.' After a while this feeling becomes intensified, and the Koan seems so overwhelming and impenetrable that the disciple is likened to a mosquito trying to bite a lump of iron, but 'at the very moment the iron absolutely rejects your frail proboscis, you for once forget yourself; you penetrate, and the work is done'. There is no way of explaining this moment other than by saying that it is the time when the fetters of illusion snap asunder at the intense pressure of the disciple's will. The Koan exercise is so devised as to concentrate the mind and stimulate the will to the highest degree, and in its later stages effort will be provoked simply by the increasing difficulty of the task. Thus when the final dilemma is faced the disciple will meet it with his entire strength, and as the tremendous force of his will meets with the stubborn resistance of the Koan, something happens; just at the moment of 'impact' when the mosquito jabs at the lump of iron, there comes the flash of Satori, and the disciple realizes that there was nothing in it after all! 'Nothing is left to you at this moment,' writes a master, 'but to burst out into a loud laugh.'

Our only means of discovering the why and wherefore of this experience is to turn to the sayings of the Zen masters themselves, and to see if we can gather anything from their descriptions of the ways in which it came upon them. A good example comes from Hakuin, who describes this last stage of the Koan exercise as follows: 'When the disciple grapples with a Koan single-handedly, he will come to see that he has reached the limit of his mental tension, and he is brought to a standstill. Like the man hanging over the precipice, he is completely at a loss what to do next. . . . All of a sudden he finds his mind and body wiped out of existence, together with the Koan. This is what is known as "letting go your hold." As you become awakened from the stupor and regain your breath, it is like drinking water and knowing for yourself that

The Technique of Zen

it is cold. It will be a joy inexpressible.' The important phrase in this quotation is 'letting go your hold'. For if the Koan is taken to be a way of presenting in miniature the giant Koan of life, the great dilemma and problem at which every being is working, however unconsciously, then, in the same way as life itself, the Koan can never be grasped. The Zen masters distinguished between two kinds of phrases (*chü*)—the dead and the living—the dead being those which were amenable to logical analysis and solution, and the living being those which could never be confined to any fixed system of interpretation. Koans belong to the second type, for they share in life's elusiveness and indefinability. Thus when the disciple comes to the final point where the Koan absolutely refuses to be grasped, he comes also to the realization that life can never be grasped, never possessed or made to stay still. Whereupon he 'lets go', and this letting go is the acceptance of life *as* life, as that which cannot be made anyone's property, which is always free and spontaneous and unlimited. The Koan is a way of presenting the central problem of life in an intensified form. For the final impasse of the Koan, of the living phrase, magnifies the impasse always reached by those who try to clutch anything that is alive in their desire that it may be possessed and made to surrender its own life to theirs. Yet they can never take hold of its life; all that they can have is its corpse, which must in time decay also. Therefore the Zen disciple is given something which cannot be killed by definition and analysis; he must try to grasp it alive, and the moment he realizes, finally and absolutely, that it cannot be grasped, he lets go, understanding in a flash what a fool he has been to deny the right of all things to live by trying to grasp them for his own. Thus at this moment he attains freedom of the spirit, for he realizes the suffering inherent in man's

75

attempt to shut the wind in a box, to keep life alive without letting it live.

There are, of course, various degrees of Satori, and in order to reach the highest of these it is necessary to work with many Koans. There are said to be 1,700 of these Koans and though it will hardly be necessary for the disciple to solve all of them before his understanding of Zen is complete, it is exceedingly rare that one alone is sufficient to achieve the final Satori. In the early stages of Zen practice the flash of enlightenment will last only for a few seconds, while as time goes on it will become more permanent, until at last the disciple has a Satori which sweeps away every shadow of doubt and uncertainty. There are certain similarities between Satori and the 'Sudden Conversion' of Christianity. William James gives some remarkable instances of this in his *Varieties of Religious Experience*, and it is interesting to compare them with the records left by the Zen masters. James gives an instance of a man who was trying to pray, and every time he attempted to call on God he felt that something was choking him.

> Finally something said: 'Venture on the atonement, for you will die anyway if you don't.' So I made one final struggle to call on God for mercy, with the same choking and strangling, determined to finish the sentence of prayer for mercy, if I did strangle and die, and the last I remember that time was falling back on the ground with the same unseen hand on my throat. . . . When I came to the very heavens seemed to open and pour down rays of light and glory. Not for a moment only, but all day and night, floods of light and glory seemed to pour through my soul, and oh, how I was changed, and everything became new. My horses and hogs and everybody seemed changed.

James shows that in almost every case the sudden conversion

The Technique of Zen

is preceded by a feeling of acute despair and wretchedness, somewhat similar to the final impasse of the Koan. He notes that Protestant theology with its emphasis on the fundamental sinfulness and impotence of man lends itself especially to this type of experience. 'In the extreme of melancholy the self that consciously *is* can do absolutely nothing. It is completely bankrupt and without resource, and no works it can accomplish will avail.' There follows the complete surrender of the soul to God, which is in some ways similar to what Hakuin describes as 'letting go your hold'. A French Protestant, Adolphe Monod, speaking of his own experience of conversion, says, 'Renouncing then all merit, all strength, abandoning all my personal resources, and acknowledging no other title to His mercy than my own utter misery . . . I prayed as I had never yet prayed in my life.' Many converts speak of the results of this final surrender as giving them an entirely new outlook on life, whereby everything becomes transformed and made full of the Glory of God. Here it is interesting to compare the Zen masters' records of the after-effects of Satori; Hakuin says, 'It is like drinking water and knowing for yourself that it is cold. It will be a joy inexpressible,' while another master already quoted is even more emphatic, saying, 'As I looked round and up and down, the whole universe . . . appeared quite different; whatever was loathsome before . . . was seen to be nothing else but the outflow of my inmost nature, which in itself remained bright, true and transparent.' Another expresses it in a verse—

Oh, this one rare occurrence,
For which would I not be glad to give ten thousand pieces of gold!
A hat is on my head, a bundle around my loins;
And on my staff the refreshing breeze and the full moon I carry!
(*Trans.* SUZUKI.)

The Spirit of Zen

Here we see that something altogether new has been found in the monk's ordinary mushroom hat, his travelling bundle, the breeze and the moon. Again, there is the story of master Yao-shan—

> One eve he climbed
> Straight up the solitary peak;
> Revealed in the clouds the moon he saw,
> And what a hearty laugh he gave!
>
> (*Trans.* SUZUKI.)

Once more we are reminded of P'ang-yün's

> How wondrously supernatural,
> And how miraculous, this!
> I draw water, and I carry fuel!

Turning from Zen to Christianity we find something closely akin to this in another record quoted by James:

> I plead for mercy, and had a vivid realization of forgiveness and renewal of my nature. ɾWhen rising from my knees I exclaimed, 'Old things have passed away, all things have become new.' It was like entering another world, a new state of existence. Natural objects were glorified, my spiritual vision was so clarified that I saw beauty in every material object of the universe, the woods were vocal with heavenly music.

But the Zen masters are more subtle and reserved in their allusions to the joy of their new life; for some reason they do not appear to be so serious about it as the Christian mystics, and only rarely do they speak of their rapture at finding so priceless a treasure. They will describe quite vividly the one moment's flash of illumination which seems to shake the whole universe, but as to what follows they only hint, and speak of it in the most matter-of-fact terms. Thus Chao-pien writes of it as

A sudden clash of thunder, the mind-doors burst open,
And lo, there sitteth the old man (the Buddha-nature) in all his homeliness.

And thereafter they refer to their realization in terms of the most ordinary affairs, for their object is to show Zen as something perfectly natural, as intimately related to everyday life, while the Buddha is just 'the old man in all his homeliness'; he has been there all the time, for his home is ordinary life, but nobody recognizes him!

There is a famous Zen parable which fitly sums up this particular attitude to life. It is said that to those who know nothing of Zen mountains are just mountains, trees are just trees, and men are just men. After one has studied Zen for a little time, the emptiness and transcience of all forms is perceived, and mountains are no longer mountains, trees no longer trees, and men no longer men, for while ignorant people believe in the reality of objective things, the partially enlightened see that they are only appearances, that they have no abiding reality and pass away like drifting clouds. But, the parable concludes, to him who has a full understanding of Zen mountains are once again mountains, trees are trees, and men are men.

Thus while the main characteristics of Satori and Sudden Conversion are the same, they are approached and interpreted in very different ways. In the first place, Conversion is held to come to essentially depraved Man from an external God, while Satori is the realization of one's own inmost nature. Conversion takes place when something comes from outside and transforms the world, while Satori is just seeing the world as it really is, for to Zen the supernatural is natural, while to Christianity it is something not inherent in nature at all; it is at certain times brought *to* nature by the Grace of God; heaven comes down to earth and supersedes nature. But in Zen there is no dualism of heaven and earth, natural and supernatural, Man and God, material and spiritual, mortal and immortal, for ordinary men and Buddhas, Samsara and Nirvana, Avidya (Ignorance) and Bodhi (Enlightenment) are the same; it is one's own spiritual realization that makes the difference, and

> The mind is its own place, and of itself
> Can make a heaven of hell, a hell of heaven.

Therefore the mind is the key to life, for under illusion it creates confusion and when clarified it reveals the Buddha-nature. Thus in Zen, as in almost all the religions of the East, the essential task is to master the mind. This is achieved primarily through the Koan exercise, and to assist this task the Zen masters have evolved a technique of meditation or Za-zen which enables the disciple to relax the body, banish wandering thoughts and preserve his nervous energy so that he may devote his entire strength to the Koan. The elements of Za-zen were probably derived from Indian Yoga, for a similar posture is adopted and careful attention is paid to correct breathing. But the aims of Yoga and Za-zen appear to be rather different, for the Zen masters discourage the various kinds of trance which are considered so important in Yoga psychology. They point out that although certain types of trance may possibly arise, they are not the objectives of the exercise; they declare, on the contrary, that wisdom can never be found by seeking after these static and other-wordly states of consciousness, for the Chinese mind required something

The Technique of Zen

altogether more vital and practical. This is not to imply that Za-zen is right while Yoga is wrong, but that different types of mind will find Enlightenment in different ways; what may be right for the Indian is wrong for the Chinese, because the inhabitants of cold or temperate climates will require something more vigorous than the inhabitants of tropical regions, where life finds it possible to carry on with a minimum of exertion.

The aim of Za-zen is simply to release the mind from having to think about the body, and to reduce all distractions so that its whole attention may be directed to a particular task. The periods of the day set aside for Za-zen in a Zen monastery (Zendo) are thus for intense work upon the Koan, although the masters advise that the Koan should be kept in mind at all times of the day, whatever one's occupation and circumstances may be. But it must be remembered that Za-zen and the Koan are not, in themselves, the objectives of the Zen life. They are a form of spiritual gymnastics to assist in bringing about a certain experience, and when that experience has been attained, the devices used for producing it can be discarded. For the aim of Zen is not to retire for ever from the world into solitary meditation; such retirement is only a means of obtaining knowledge, which, to be of any use, must be applied to the Bodhisattva's task of bringing wisdom to all the world. To confuse this objective with sitting in Za-zen and working at Koans is once again to mistake the finger for the moon, thereby defeating entirely the purpose of these exercises. As is said in the commentary to the Cowherding Pictures, 'When you know that what you need is not the snare or the net, but the hare and the fish, it is like gold separated from dross, like the moon rising out of the clouds.'

Life in a Zen Community

The Buddha's first action after his Enlightenment was to found his Order (Sangha) of homeless mendicants—wandering sages who had sacrificed all for learning and spreading the Law, begging their means of livelihood from those to whom they preached, and living in the greatest simplicity with no other possessions than 'one robe and one bowl, under a tree and on a stone'. Originally they were not ascetics who stinted themselves as a penance; they did not regard simplicity as an end in itself, but merely as a means of relieving themselves of all encumbrances so that their whole energy might be directed to the one important task of finding Enlightenment for themselves and for others. Not long after the Buddha's death these homeless mendicants began to gather together in monastic communities, and as the years went by their numbers increased rapidly; communities (*viharas*) began to spring up all over India, spreading in time to Ceylon, Tibet and China, and to this day the members of the Sangha may be found over the whole of Eastern Asia, in the Hawaiian Islands and even in Western America.

Needless to say, Buddhism did not escape from any of the evils of monasticism. The original ideal of the monk (*bhikku*) was very high; his social function was the important task of acting as 'guide, philosopher and friend' to the community, in return for which he was supported by gifts of food. Because the principles of Buddhism inculcated the greatest reverence for all things in the universe, he was careful to use everything given to him to its fullest extent so that nothing might be wasted; his clothes were supposed to be cast-off rags, and even when these fell to pieces some goodness was still to be found in them for they were made into mops to clean out the vihara. All things were of value, and nothing might be despised, nothing cast away if it were still capable of being used. But if an institution which maintains itself by begging is to retain its original purity for long, its members must be highly developed beings, and as these are few and far between the Buddhist monks tended to become lazy and degenerate, living on the community as parasites pandering to the superstitions of ignorant folk. Monasteries became rich with the gifts of princes and wealthy merchants, until the monk's home of 'under a tree and on a stone' became in many places a vast and highly adorned palace. Cast-off rags became gorgeous robes of silk, while the heads of monasteries assumed all the dignity and even the power of temporal rulers. These developments were not without redeeming features, for the increasing richness of the monastic communities enabled their members to produce magnificent works of art to which the imagery and symbolism of Buddhism lent itself with great ease.

By the Sixth Century A.D. the monastic Buddhism of China had reached a high stage of development, and the records say that there were communities numbering each a thousand or more monks, somewhat similar to the enormous monasteries to be found in Tibet and Mongolia at the present time, many of which are cities in themselves. From the beginning the Zen Patriarchs began to gather these communities about them, and just as Zen gave a new lift to the teachings of Buddhism, so also it gave a new life to monastic institutions. The evolution of the Zen community as it exists to-day must be dated from the time of the master Po-chang (Jap. Hyakujo), who died in

Life in a Zen Community

A.D. 814. Po-chang recognized the need for establishing monastic institutions of a rather different kind from any that had hitherto existed, for while the communities of the time had become contemplative and other-worldly it was essential to the Zen life that it should be in close touch with the ordinary labours of the world. If society was to be assisted in applying Buddhism to its everyday life little could be achieved if the recognized teachers of Buddhism were altogether removed from that life. Therefore Po-chang drew up a set of rules and precepts for a distinctively Zen community, and this work, known as the *Po-chang Ching-kuei*, has formed the basis of the monastic life of Zen Buddhism ever afterwards.

Po-chang saw at once that if monastic life was to retain its vitality, it was essential that the monks should not live by begging alone. Thus the first principle of his regulations was that 'a day of no working is a day of no eating', and for this reason almost every Zen community is attached to a farm where rice and other vegetables are grown for the needs of the brotherhood. He insisted that every member of the community must undertake some kind of labour, for Zen finds nothing degrading in even the most menial types of manual work, so much so that new-comers to the monastery are as a rule given lighter and more attractive tasks than the monks of higher rank. Every institution is, as far as possible, self-contained and democratically governed; it has its own cooks, secretarial staff, administrators, proctors, builders, craftsmen and sextons, and while the master attached to each monastery has no particular part to play in the government and administration of the community, he shares with its members in all the ordinary labours required for its maintenance.

The life of the community centres round the Meditation Hall (Semmon Dojo)—a large rectangular building, varying

85

in size according to the number of monks—and it is here that the inmates practise their Za-zen, keep their few belongings and sleep at nights. Apart from this there is the dining-hall, kitchen, lavatories, sick-rooms, the master's private apartments, the garden, and frequently woods and fields, besides a number of special offices and guest-rooms. Professor Suzuki has recently (1934) published a work on *The Training of the Zen Buddhist Monk* which is illustrated by a remarkable series of pictures by Zenchu Sato, who is a member of a large community at Kamakura. These pictures do not pretend to have any great artistic value, but they give a very definite impression of the *esprit de corps* of a Zen monastery, and one of the most noticeable things about them is the happiness and jollity of the monks as they go about their various tasks. Whether they are chopping wood, cooking the meals, washing clothes or shaving, there are laughing faces and obvious signs of great industry. In fact, the industry of Zen monks has become proverbial, and in Japan when someone's house is said to be like a Zen monastery it means that it is scrupulously clean and tidy. To guard against the dangers of libertinism, life is regulated with a strict discipline; all important functions are carried out with precision and regularity, so much so that they appear to be ceremonies. Waste of both time and material is reduced to a minimum, and the monk's possessions are so few that they are just enough to make a pillow for him to sleep on at night. But this is not because the ideal of Zen is asceticism; Zen is no more asceticism than it is any other *form* of life, for Zen is an attitude towards life, and as such it believes in using just the right amount of time, energy and material required to achieve a given object—no more and no less.

While some of the Zen monasteries in Japan are treasure houses of both Chinese and Japanese works of art—paintings,

Life in a Zen Community

pottery, bronzes, lacquer and carved wood—these objects are not displayed with the same profusion that is found in the temples of other sects. The decoration of a Zen monastery is, as a rule, carried out with the same spirit of economy which prevails in the discipline and ceremonial. The aim is that each work of art shall be fully appreciated, and this is impossible if too many are displayed at a time. Thus the prevailing atmosphere of a Zen monastery is one of severe simplicity, relieved here and there by carefully selected objects of great beauty; but this simplicity must not be taken to mean the mere absence of adornment. Zen has so influenced architecture and the art of furnishing that the very structure of rooms is beautiful in itself apart from any additional ornamentation. Thus the subtly tinted paper screens (*shoji*) which form the walls of a Japanese room, the wooden frames upon which they are stretched, the dull yellow of the rice-straw mats (*tatami*) on the floor, and the long, low, expansive lines of the buildings have an indefinable, quiet beauty of their own even though made of the simplest and most inexpensive materials. The Meditation Hall itself is such a room as this, its own object of adornment being the shrine of the Buddha (*Butsudan*) standing in the centre of the Hall with perhaps just a single spray of flowers set before it. The Hall itself is long and narrow, panelled on either side with plain *shoji* of a faint greyish tint, concealing entrances into the surrounding courtyards or gardens and cupboards where the monks keep their bedding. Parallel to the walls down either side of the Hall are low platforms upon which the monks sleep and practise their Za-zen. At the time of meditation they come into the Hall in procession and take their seats on these platforms facing the centre of the room. The head monk goes forward and prostrates himself before the shrine, while outside another monk summons

87

any members of the community who happen to be late by beating on a flat wooden gong bearing the inscription:

> Birth and death is a grave event;
> How transient is life!
> Every minute is to be grudged,
> Time waits for nobody.

The head monk then lights a stick of incense to mark the time, and when he has returned to his seat Za-zen begins. At this point two other monks rise from their seats and approach the shrine, bowing to each other and to the figure of a Bodhisattva, whereupon each takes up a flat, tapering piece of wood (*keisaku*), and after a further bow they separate and go to opposite sides of the Hall. Then they begin to walk backwards and forwards in front of the two rows of meditating monks, keeping a careful look out for anyone who shows signs of drowsiness. At first they walk swiftly, but after a while they slow down their pace, treading more and more softly until they move like shadows. Suddenly one of them stops before a monk who appears to be sleepy, and giving him a few sharp slaps across the shoulders with the *keisaku*, restores him at once to full consciousness. After a while they return to their seats, and meditation continues until the stick of incense has burnt down to the end, whereupon the head monk sounds a bell and strikes together two wooden clappers. This is the signal for relaxation and exercise, and at once the *shoji* are pushed aside to let in the air. Then, falling into a column, the monks begin to march swiftly and quietly round the Hall, gathering speed as they go, and when another stick of incense has burnt down the head monk strikes the clappers again. Refreshed by their exercise the monks return to meditation, and these periods of Za-zen and exercise continue for some three hours until it is time for the principal meal of the day, which takes place at ten o'clock.

Every monk keeps a nest of small eating-bowls in a wooden box, wrapped in a napkin. At meal times he takes these out of his cupboard in the Hall and proceeds to the dining-room where long wooden tables, standing about a foot from the ground, have been prepared. The Zen monk has three meals a day—breakfast at a little after four o'clock in the morning, the principal meal at ten, and what is known as 'medicinal food' at five. Members of the Sangha are not supposed to eat after the middle of the day, but since climatic conditions in Japan will not allow this, the afternoon meal is called 'medicinal', being composed of what is left over from the meal at ten. In a Zen monastery the eating of food is attended with a special ceremonial which begins with the recitation of a short sutra, followed by the 'Five Meditations on Eating':[1]

Firstly, let us reflect on our own work, let us see whence comes this offering of food;

Secondly, let us reflect how imperfect our virtue is, whether we deserve this offering;

Thirdly, what is most essential is to hold our minds in control and be detached from the various faults;

Fourthly, that this is medicinal and is taken to keep our bodies in good health;

Fifthly, in order to accomplish the task of Enlightenment, we accept this food.

(*Trans.* SUZUKI.)

When this recitation is finished, two monks come forward with a great wooden bowl of rice which they serve out to the

[1] The ideas expressed in this and other 'recitations' quoted are not peculiar to Zen. They have been adopted by the Zen monks as part of the usual ceremonial used in Buddhist monasteries in the Far East.

company, followed by another monk who hands out pickled vegetables. Another serves tea, and when all have been given their food, each sets a small portion of his meal on the edge of the wooden table as an offering to the unseen spirits, saying:

> O you of the spiritual worlds,
> I now offer this to you;
> Let this food fill the ten quarters
> And all the spirits enjoy it.
>
> (*Trans.* SUZUKI.)

Afterwards these offerings are taken outside for the birds. As they eat the monks continue to meditate on the principles of Buddhism—

> The first morsel is to destroy all evils,
> The second morsel is to practise all good deeds,
> The third morsel is to save all sentient beings—
> May we all attain the path of Buddhahood.
>
> (*Trans.* SUZUKI.)

The repast is continued in silence, while the attendants give second helpings to those who signify that they want more by folding their arms before them; those who have had enough simply rub their hands together as the attendant passes. Not a scrap of food is left in the bowls, which are cleaned by pouring the remainder of the tea from one to the other, swilling it round and finally drinking it. They are then wiped with the napkin and replaced in their boxes, to the accompaniment of a further recitation:

Having finished this meal, my bodily strength is fully restored;
My power extends over the ten quarters and through the three periods
    of time, and I am a strong man;

Life in a Zen Community

As to reversing the wheel of cause and effect, no thought is to be
wasted over it.
May all beings attain miraculous powers!

(*Trans.* SUZUKI.)

Or alternatively:

As the skies are limitless, so shall be my compassion to all sentient
beings.
The mind released should be free and unclinging to things of the
earth.
As the flowers of the lotus are lovely and unstained, rising up from
the mud, so shall my meditations be even though living in this
world of illusion.
With mind so purified I offer homage to the Buddha, the Enlightened
One.

Twice a day the master of the monastery holds interviews
with the monks to find out how they are progressing with their
Koans and to give personal instruction. These interviews are
known as San-zen, and are attended voluntarily. The great
bulk of written teachings on Zen consists of records of such
interviews as these, several of which have already been quoted.
The monk is ushered into the master's room with all due
observance of monastic conventions; there is much bowing
and ringing of bells, but as soon as the interview begins conventions are altogether set aside. Thus the master may begin
by asking the monk some question, frequently the Koan on
which he has been working. Thus Shih-kung asked:

'Can you take hold of empty space?'

'Yes, sir,' replied the monk.

'Show me how you do it.'

The monk made a clutching movement in the air with his
hand, but Shih-kung exclaimed:

'Is that the way? But after all you have not got anything.'

Therefore the monk asked, 'What, then, is your way?'

Immediately Shih-kung took hold of the monk's nose, and, giving it a sharp pull, called out:

'That is the way to have good hold of empty space!' Or it may be that the monk will open the interview by asking the master a question, as for instance:

'What do you say when I come to you with nothing?'

'Fling it down to the ground.'

'I said that I had nothing, what shall I let go?'

'If so, take it away.'

Even to hold on to the idea that Zen is to possess nothing is to miss the truth.

Shih-kung's pulling of his disciple's nose is no unusual behaviour in these interviews, but this is neither madness nor brutality; in so far as it is possible to give a *rational* explanation of it, its meaning is to demonstrate Zen by some very positive action, showing that Zen is actual living reality. Mere obscure words or strange movements might be interpreted as symbolism, but about a smack on the face there can be no mistake; here is something thoroughly alive, so quick that it cannot be grasped, so emphatic that there can be no 'philosophizing' about it. Words can be written down; they can be depended upon to stay still and imagined to contain the truth, but a smack is a smack—once given it cannot be called back nor analysed nor used as a means of trying to confine truth to a permanent formula. Thus when someone says, 'Zen is to see into one's own nature,' here is something one can hold on to as expressing the truth of Zen, yet that is to miss it altogether. But when the master just gives a smack one cannot hold on to it at all, and for that reason he has really expressed the truth of Zen.

Sometimes the master of a monastery will give a more

Life in a Zen Community

formal kind of instruction than San-zen. This is the *teisho*—a discourse on the inner meaning of one of the Zen text-books, when the master addresses the whole community gathered together. These discourses are usually given at the time of year when Za-zen is practised more frequently than usual; that is to say, during the weeks when some important event in the life of the Buddha is being commemorated. These periods are known as *Sesshin*, and the monks rise at two in the morning instead of at four, spending almost the whole day in the Meditation Hall. San-zen is held more frequently, and less time is devoted to the ordinary work of running the monastery, which usually occupies most of the day. The giving of a *teisho* is attended with much ceremonial and sutra recitation. The monks put on a special robe and go to the lecture hall in a solemn procession; the master arrives shortly afterwards accompanied by two attendants, and having made his obeisance before the image of the Buddha he takes his seat on a high chair, before which a reading-desk has been placed. Then he may read a passage from the Zen records, stopping to explain various points, or else he may deliver a Zen 'sermon'. If it should be the latter, unusual things are wont to happen. One day a master had just taken his seat when outside a bird began to sing. The master said nothing and everyone listened to the bird. When the song stopped the master simply announced that the sermon had been preached and went away. On another occasion the master stretched out his arms and remained silent. He was about to leave the hall when one of the monks asked him why he had said nothing, to which he answered, 'The scriptures are expounded by the scripture teachers and the commentaries by the commentators. Why, then, do you wonder at me? Am I not a Zen teacher?' Master I-tuan once said to his assembled monks, 'To talk is blaspheming, to remain silent is deception. Beyond silence and talking there is an upward passage, but my mouth is not wide enough to point it out to you.' So saying, he left the hall. Sometimes monks will come forward with questions, or else the master will ask one of them to demonstrate his understanding of Zen. Thus master Shou-shan began his discourse by producing a stick and asking, 'Call this a stick and you assert; call it not a stick and you negate. Now, do not assert or negate, and what would you call it? Speak! Speak!' Whereupon a monk came out of the assembly, seized the stick and broke it in two, asking, 'What is this?' All these strange utterances must be treated in the same way as the Koan; sometimes they contain obscure symbolism or references to the sayings of other masters which only learned students of Zen literature can understand, but these are only superficial difficulties. Intellectual analysis may reveal a fraction of their meaning, but essentially they are like smooth balls of steel. The harder the sword of intellect cuts at them, the faster do they jump away.

At the conclusion of the master's discourse the monks recite the 'Four Great Vows' before returning to the Meditation Hall—

> However innumerable sentient beings are,
>   I vow to save them;
> However inexhaustible the passions are,
>   I vow to extinguish them;
> However immeasurable the Dharmas are,
>   I vow to study them;
> However incomparable the Buddha-truth is,
>   I vow to attain it.
>
> (*Trans.* SUZUKI.)

Apart from these specifically religious and ceremonial

Life in a Zen Community

activities which have been described, the life of the Zen monk is occupied principally by the work of maintaining the monastery. But in Zen this too might be called specifically religious, for from the standpoint of Buddha-nature no one activity is more religious or holy than any other. Therefore Zen finds religion in everyday activities, laying particular emphasis on this finding, for the general rule is for men to seek religion apart from ordinary life. In the words of George Herbert,

> All may of Thee partake;
> Nothing can be so mean
> Which with this tincture, 'For Thy sake,'
> Will not grow bright and clean.

> A servant with this clause
> Makes drudgery divine.
> Who sweeps a room as for Thy laws
> Makes that and the action fine.

This is pure Zen, except that Buddhists would say that they work not for God's sake, but for the Enlightenment of all sentient beings. Yet after all there is hardly so much difference as that between the two, for sentient beings are essentially the Buddha-nature, and to serve them is to serve the highest principle in the universe, to work in harmony with the supreme law of life which is that all beings are potentially Buddhas and that at some time they must become so in actuality. Jesus, too, said that on the Last Day God would say to His children, 'Inasmuch as ye have done it unto one of the least of these My brethren, *ye have done it unto Me.*'

There are innumerable references in the literature of Zen to the discovery of Enlightenment in the ordinary work of life.

Tai-an asked Po-chang, 'I have been seeking for the Buddha, but do not yet know how to go on with my research.'

Po-chang replied, 'It is very much like looking for an ox when you are riding on one.'

'What shall a man do after knowing him?'

'It is like going home on the back of an ox.'

'May I be further enlightened as to the care I shall have to bestow on the whole matter?'

'It is like a cowherd,' said Po-chang, 'looking after his cattle, who using his staff keeps them from wandering into another's pasture.'

When master Chao-chou was sweeping one of the rooms in his monastery a disciple asked him, 'You are a great Zen master free from the dust of evil thoughts, and why this busy sweeping?' Immediately the master replied, 'The dust comes from outside!' One day a master approached the keeper of the monastery granary while he was sifting rice through a sieve. The master said,

'Don't scatter the grains, for they come from our kind-hearted donors.'

'No, master, I won't scatter them about.'

The master saw a single grain of rice lying on the ground, and, picking it up, asked, 'You say you don't scatter them about; if so, where does this grain come from?'

The keeper said nothing, so the master spoke again:

'Be careful not to think slightingly of this one grain of rice, for hundreds of thousands of grains all come out of it.'

In conclusion it should be made clear that not every Zen monk desires to remain for ever in a monastery. Having qualified as a master he may or may not take charge of another community; in many cases he will return to the ordinary life of the world, or else become a wandering teacher of the Law, travelling from place to place and helping those whom he meets by the way. For the ideal of the Bodhisattva is not to remain apart from the world; it is to be in it, though not of it, to be an anonymous force for Enlightenment working in and through human society. If he has any solitude it is the solitude which inevitably attaches itself to great wisdom. He cannot isolate himself from other beings, for in every creature he sees one of his other selves. Therefore if there is any isolation it is by reason of the barriers which others erect against him through fear of or indifference to his wisdom. It is not the selfish isolation of the hermit who tries to gain spiritual freedom through physical freedom, for the Bodhisattva knows that the two are independent of each other. A man may be free to travel where he likes, but there is no place on earth where he can escape from his own Karma, and whether he lives on a mountain or in a city he may still be the victim of an uncontrolled mind. For man's Karma travels with him, like his shadow. Indeed, it is his shadow, for it has been said, 'Man stands in his own shadow and wonders why it is dark.'

Zen and the Civilization
of the Far East

The ultimate test of any religion is its effect upon the lives of its followers, for 'by their fruits ye shall know them'. There is, however, a tendency to judge these effects differently in the West than in the East, for Europeans will test the value of a religion by the success it achieves in bringing harmony into society as a whole, by the extent to which it improves the social condition of the masses, and by its capacity to reach and be understood by 'all sorts and conditions of men'. But the religions of Asia were not originally intended to be 'mass religions', where they have become so they are altogether different from the forms in which they were first taught, for the East regards wisdom not as something to be handed out indiscriminately to all and sundry, but as the right of the few who show themselves capable of understanding and applying it in the correct way. In the West we have a saying that 'Knowledge is Power', and yet we take great pains to convey this power to all people, irrespective of their fitness to be trusted with it. Thus whatever benefits may be derived from the wide distribution of knowledge, they are overbalanced by the terrible abuses of knowledge which lie at the root of nearly all the great problems of modern civilization. Nobody would dream of allowing a child to play with the switches in an electric power-house, and yet the wisdom of the West, which is Science, can become anyone's property, whatever his motives for wishing to possess it may be. Perhaps the West is

now beginning to regret its wise men's liberality with their knowledge, for in the last half-century we have seen physical science exploited for all kinds of destructive, immoral and anti-social ends. At the same time the West has hospitals, hygienic sanitation and other material blessings which are altogether new to the East; yet it has to pay for them dearly when the two-edged blade of knowledge cuts the other way.

The wisdom of the East is not physical but psychic and spiritual Science, and while the results of abusing physical Science are bad enough, the abuse of psychic and spiritual Science is immeasurably worse because it wrecks far more than men's bodies. Fortunately the wise men of the East have chosen their disciples carefully and have veiled their deepest knowledge in myths and symbols understandable only by those whom they see fit to trust. Therefore Westerners have often accused them of jealousy, of selfishly hiding their wisdom from the masses for fear that their own supremacy would be endangered if the whole world were to discover their secrets. But this is not so; the reason for their secrecy is that they have a far greater respect and reverence for wisdom than is usual in the West, for while we spread our wisdom abroad as if it were some cheap news item, they regard it as the most priceless of all treasures. In order to obtain it a man must sacrifice all that he has; he must be prepared to go to any lengths to show that he really does desire to learn and to make good use of his knowledge; in short he must prove that he values wisdom above all other things, that he regards it as a sacred trust never to be used for unworthy ends. It was for this reason that Shang Kwang had to cut off his arm after waiting for a week in the snow before Bodhidharma would see him.

Yet the foregoing in no way conflicts with what has been said about the truth of Zen being revealed in ordinary life, or with the fact that it is perfectly clear for those who have eyes to see. For the great treasure which cannot be had without so much sacrifice is not Truth itself; that is to be found every-where—with everyone and everything, whether its presence is realized or not; it is no more the property of wise men than of fools and lunatics, for the Buddha-nature is common to all. The rare treasure is the capacity to see Truth. Thus, like every other Eastern religion in its highest expression, Zen is for the few, though it differs from other forms of Buddhism, from Hinduism and Taoism, in that it has never had an exoteric or popular form. Therefore the immediate effects of Zen upon the civilization of the Far East must not be sought in the life of the masses except in so far as this was affected by rulers and administrators who had come into contact with the Zen masters. The effects of Zen will be found in the life and work of certain individuals and of various small groups of people, such as the samurai or warrior class of feudal Japan. In the East the effectiveness of a religion is judged by its success in producing a comparatively small number of thoroughly enlightened men, for it is not believed possible fundamentally to alter the lives of vast numbers of people within the span of a thousand years or so. Great social changes are not expected; the religions of the East are more concerned with the en-lightenment of some few individuals than of society as a whole, because society is made up of individuals, and will only be-come enlightened when, after thousands of years, more and more individuals have proved themselves fit for the highest knowledge, until the chosen few have become the whole community.

In the history of the Far East the fruits of Zen are several hundred characters of such remarkable greatness that by them-selves they would be sufficient witness to the value of Zen,

The Spirit of Zen

artistic achievements which equal anything produced at any other time or place in the world, a form of chivalry and military technique with good claim to be unsurpassed, and a sure foundation of experience for future work on a far greater scale. It is, of course, particularly difficult to give accurate descriptions of the characters of the great Zen masters and devotees, for their greatness was less in what they said or did than in what they were, and in the impression which they created upon those who came into contact with them. While it is true that many of them were superb artists or warriors of tremendous courage, their essential qualities were like Zen itself—unmistakable but quite indefinable. We must gather our own impressions of them from the accounts of their ways of teaching and from the pictures of them which have been left to us by artists deeply imbued with the spirit of Zen. As to the accounts of their teachings, many of these have been quoted; in all there is something forceful, spontaneous and unhesitating. They waste no words; they avoid all forms of pedantry, and in answering questions they never evade the real issue by an abstract discourse, but say something which goes right to the heart of the questioner, touching him personally in a way that may be unintelligible to others. So keen is their intuition of another person's state of mind that they are never taken in by those who try to deceive them with a second-hand knowledge of Zen. Master Chu-hung was once writing a book on the ten laudable deeds of a monk, when one of these pretenders asked him, 'What is the use of writing such a book when in Zen there is not even an atom of a thing to be called laudable or not?' 'The five aggregates of personality are entangling,' replied the master, 'and the four elements grow rampant, and how can you say there are no evils?' 'The four elements,' countered the other, 'are ultimately all empty and the five aggregates have no reality whatever.' This remark elicited a slap on the face, with the reproof, 'So many are mere learned ones; you are not the real thing yet. Give me another answer.' The monk was furious, and making no answer he was about to go away when the master smiled at him and said, 'There, why don't you wipe the dirt off your own face?'

There is a remarkable triptych by the Japanese painter Jasoku, showing Bodhidharma, Lin-chi and Te-shan—three of the greatest exponents of Zen. The portrait of Bodhidharma is of the head and shoulders alone, loosely draped with a flowing wrap, which covers his head and falls over his shoulders, showing just the face and chest. The easy lines of the wrap contrast sharply with his powerful features, prominent eyebrows, a rough moustache reaching from below his aquiline nose to the extremities of a great square jaw, fringed with a short bushy beard. But the whole force of the picture is concentrated in the eyes. They look slightly upwards and to one side, with lids wide open, and with steady, penetrating gaze he seems to be watching intently at something just over one's head. Bodhidharma is sometimes referred to as the 'Bearded Barbarian,' yet in spite of the huge moustache, shaggy eyebrows and unkempt beard there is something in Jasoku's picture essentially aristocratic. Here is no contemplative, dreamy Buddhism; the artist has made Bodhidharma personify the dynamic and positive spontaneity of life. The same is true of his portrait of Lin-chi. Here the master is shown sitting in the posture of meditation with his hands clasped on his lap, and from beneath a high, smooth forehead, the same powerful and penetrating eyes are watching. Yet in spite of his almost fierce countenance, the picture

gives an unmistakable impression of the deepest calm and
gentleness. For there was this paradox in the characters of all
the Zen masters—the immovable equanimity and boundless
compassion of the Bodhisattva, combined with a vitality as
brilliant and ruthless as lightning. This paradox reflected itself
in other ways, and in Japan we find the followers of Zen
embracing the two seemingly incompatible parts of poet and
soldier, lofty idealist and grim realist. When master So-gen
was about to be beheaded by a gang of ruffians, he quietly sat
down and wrote this verse:

> The heaven and earth afford me no shelter at all;
> I'm glad, unreal are body and soul.
> Welcome thy weapon, O warrior of Yuan! Thy trusty steel,
> That flashes lightning, cuts the wind of Spring, I feel.
>
> (*Trans.* NUKARIYA.)

So also the great fencing master, Miyamoto Musashi:

> Under the sword lifted high,
> There is hell making you tremble;
> But go ahead,
> And you have the land of bliss.
>
> (*Trans.* SUZUKI.)

Just as we find these two distinct elements in the characters of
the Zen masters and their disciples, so do we find that Zen has
influenced the civilization of the Far East in two directions—in
aesthetics and in the military arts. On the one hand it was Zen
which produced the poetry and other-worldliness of the tea-
ceremony (*cha-no-yu*), the art of landscape gardening, the work
of the Sung, Sumiye and Kano painters, the poetry of Basho
and the quiet simplicity of Japanese architecture, while on the
other it was Zen which produced the alarming technique of
ju-jutsu and *kenjutsu* (fencing), and the stern principles of

bushido—the Samurai's code of chivalry.[1] Thus the paradox of Zen was that it could combine the peace of Nirvana with the intense activity of battle and the common tasks of everyday life. To quote Takuan once again,

> What is most important is to acquire a certain mental attitude known as 'immovable wisdom.' . . . 'Immovable' does not mean to be stiff and heavy and lifeless as a rock or piece of wood. It means the highest degree of mobility with a centre which remains immovable. The mind then reaches the highest point of alacrity ready to direct its attention anywhere it is needed. . . . There is something immovable within, which, however, moves along spontaneously with things presenting themselves before it. The mirror of wisdom reflects them instantaneously one after another, keeping itself intact and undisturbed.

In the realm of aesthetics the first important traces of Zen influence are found in the art of the T'ang Dynasty (A.D. 618–905). At some time during the latter half of this period lived the greatest of all Chinese painters, Wu Tao-tzu. Unfortunately all of his work is now lost to us with the exception of one superb triptych, and many authorities hold that even this is a copy. This painting is to be found in one of the Zen monasteries at Kyoto, and shows the Buddha with the two great Bodhisattvas, Manjusri and Samantabhadra; it is the central figure of the Buddha which holds one's gaze. Contemporaries describe the artist as painting 'as if a whirlwind possessed his hand' and its influence will certainly be seen if one looks into the details of this central figure. The lines forming the folds of the Buddha's robe are sharp, bold and jagged, but the face bears an expression of such absolute serenity that it

[1] For the influence of Zen on the poetry and drama of Japan, see Mr E. V. Gatenby's *Cloud Men of Yamato*—also in this series.

dominates the whole picture, making it a symbol of the spirit of Zen; it is intense liveliness with a foundation of complete rest. As the Taoists would say, 'Just because the axle moves not, the spokes revolve,' or, 'It is the principle of non-action that makes all things move.' The same characteristics are found in the paintings of the Japanese school of Sumiye. These pictures were executed on a particular type of rough and brittle paper with a soft brush. The medium was black Chinese ink; there was no colouring, no elaboration, and the effect of the brittle paper was that a stroke once made could never be effaced, while if it were not to smudge it must be drawn swiftly and deftly. With such materials it was absolutely necessary for the artist to paint 'as if a whirlwind possessed his hand'; there was no possibility of 'touching up'; the least error made itself obvious, and if the artist were to stop and think in the middle of his stroke the result would be an ugly blot. This technique was exactly suited to the spirit of Zen, for it implied that the artist must commit his inspiration to paper while it was still alive; he could not make a rough sketch and then slowly fill in the details, until the inspiration was killed by a mass of changes and elaborations. He must make the picture complete in a few moments, for it was like the Zen master's slap on the face— sudden, irrevocable, definite and lively; a smack given slowly and tentatively is no smack at all but a feeble push—it has no life, no spontaneity. Similarly a picture that does not catch the inspiration while it lives but laboriously tries to resurrect it when it is dead is like a stuffed bird in a glass case; Sumiye catches the bird in a second before it has flown away—indeed, it allows it to fly away because it has no need to have it shot and stuffed so that the artist can examine its corpse at leisure. Thus the Sumiye artist must always 'Walk on!' for death follows life just one pace behind.

Zen and Civilization of Far East

Yet for all the suddenness and immediacy of Sumiye it has its underlying calm, and that is in the elimination of non-essentials. This principle is much earlier than Sumiye, for it goes back to the very beginnings of Zen and further into the philosophy of Taoism, where it was taught as 'economy of force'. In the *Tao Te Ching* it is said:

> A violent wind does not outlast the morning; a squall of rain does not outlast the day. Such is the course of Nature. And if Nature herself cannot sustain her efforts long, how much less can man!

And again:

> The skilful traveller leaves no tracks; the skilful speaker makes no blunders.
>
> (*Trans.* LIONEL GILES.)

For the good walker uses just the right amount of energy to move himself along; leaving no tracks he walks light and so raises no dust. The Taoist would say that if a walker raises dust it is a sign that he is using energy which is not absorbed in carrying out his purpose; therefore it goes elsewhere and is wasted in stirring up the dust. While this analogy may be somewhat far-fetched, the basic principle is the secret of concentration and of success in any form of activity. It is to use just the right amount of energy required to achieve a given result, but as a rule man makes his life more difficult than it need be by wasting an enormous amount of his strength in every task that he undertakes. In the first place, the total energy expended is greater than what is required to achieve the task, and in the second, only a small portion of it is actually absorbed in that task because it is scattered far and wide instead of being directed at one point. Therefore master Po-chang said that Zen meant, 'Eat when you are hungry, sleep when you are

107

tired. . . . Most people do not eat but think of various other things, thereby allowing themselves to be disturbed; they do not sleep but dream of a thousand and one things.' The uncontrolled mind uses up its energy over innumerable worries, distractions and wandering ideas instead of giving itself to one thing at a time, and for this reason it never achieves completely what it sets out to do, for the moment it begins on one thing it runs off to others, exhausing itself with a tremendous amount of wasted activity. In comparison with this the activity of Taoism and Zen may appear to be inconsiderable, yet this is only because they hold strength in reserve; their calmness is the result of a one-pointed attitude of mind; they take each thing as it comes, finish with it and pass on to the next, so avoiding all the useless running backwards and forwards, worrying about the past and future, by which activity simply defeats itself.

Thus 'economy of force' is the Zen principle of 'going right ahead', and in life as well as in art Zen never wastes energy in stopping to explain; it only indicates. Just as in philosophy it points to 'the cypress tree in the courtyard' or 'the bamboo grove at the foot of the hill' without further comment, without going into any metaphysical analysis, so in art it indicates the bare essentials without elaboration. For Zen is to see life for oneself, and if the philosopher and the artist describe all that there is to be seen, their descriptions become so easily a substitute for first-hand experience. Therefore the purpose of philosophy and art is not to provide a reproduction of life in words or in paint, for the real thing is better than any reproduction. Their purpose is to give one the hint to see for oneself. Hence the Chinese artists understood better than any others the value of empty spaces, and in a certain sense what they left out was more important than what they put in; it was a tantalizing reticence, a vacuum which drew out curiosity; they lifted just a corner of the veil to excite people to find out for themselves what lay beyond. This was the Taoist principle of *wu-wei*, of arriving at action through non-action. With a few strokes of the brush the Sung artist could achieve more than others could achieve after weeks of painstaking labour, for his strength was in his 'economy of force'.

The great Zen painters of the Sung Dynasty (960–1279) were Kuo Hsi, Mi Fei, Ma Yuan and Mu Ch'i, and of these Ma Yuan was especially famed for painting just 'one corner'. A fine example of his work is the picture of the 'Solitary Angler', where in the midst of a dim nothingness a small, frail boat is seen floating on water faintly suggested by a few soft curves, while the fisherman sits at one end with his line trailing out behind. One of Mu Ch'i's masterpieces, called 'In the Morning Sun', shows no sign of the sun at all—only the dimly outlined figure of a little, bald-headed Zen monk, absorbed in plaiting a straw rope with one end tied to his big toe. The only solid part of the picture is formed by a few clumps of grass and shrubbery around the rock upon which he is sitting, against a light, hazy background suggesting the morning mist. At the end of the Sung Dynasty Zen began to die out in China, and the art of the Ming period showed tendencies towards over-elaboration and prettiness. The real tradition of Sung passed to Japan, where it was taken up by the schools of Sumiye and Kano, extending itself beyond painting to architecture, gardening and especially to the aesthetics of the tea-ceremony and all that it implied.

The drinking of tea had always been associated with Zen, and from the earliest times the monks used it to keep themselves awake during long periods of meditation. There is a gruesome legend as to its origin which tells that Bodhidharma once fell asleep during his meditations and was so furious that he cut off his eyelids. Falling to the ground they at once turned into the first tea-plants, and ever afterwards the drink made from its leaves has kept off sleep and purified the soul. The elements of the tea-ceremony were brought to Japan from China, where the Zen monks used to pass a large bowl of tea from one to another while sitting in the Meditation Hall, and the T'ang poet Luwuh in his famous work the *Cha-ching* (The Scripture of Tea) laid the foundations of the ritual and philosophy of tea. Okakura Kakuzo writes that he 'was born in an age when Buddhism, Taoism and Confucianism were seeking mutual synthesis. The pantheistic symbolism of the time was urging one to mirror the Universal in the Particular. Luwuh saw in the Tea-service the same harmony and order which reigned through all things.' Another poet of the same period said of tea:

> The first cup moistens my lips and throat, the second cup breaks my loneliness, the third cup searches my inmost being. . . . The fourth cup raises a slight perspiration—all the wrong of life passes away through my pores. At the fifth cup I am purified; the sixth cup calls me to the realms of immortals. The seventh cup—ah, but I could take no more! I only feel the breath of cool wind that rises in my sleeves. Where is Heaven? Let me ride on this sweet breeze and waft away thither.

Such were the feelings that became associated with tea-drinking, and by the time it came to Japan it was no mere commodity; it was something much more than a drink made from dried leaves, for a Zen master could say, 'Mark well that the taste of Zen (*Ch'an*) and the taste of tea (*cha*) are the same.' This was not only a pun; gradually all the aesthetic ideals of Zen had attached themselves to the ceremony of drinking tea, for while the monks used it to refresh themselves during their hard struggles with the Koan, they began to accompany it with all those things which bring quietness and peace of mind. It was not long before the practice of drinking it in the Meditation Hall was discontinued, and instead a special room was set apart for the purpose. From this evolved the Tea House (*chaseki*), the 'Abode of Emptiness', a frail paper structure with a simple roof of rice-straw, hidden away in a corner of the garden. In this way the tea-ceremony became recognized as the most satisfactory way of refreshing the spirit; essentially it was a temporary escape from all cares and distractions—a period of rest and contemplation, of absorption in all that was beautiful in nature and art.

As time went on the garden in which the Tea House was built itself became an incidental to the tea-ceremony, and the path of great flat stones which crossed the miniature landscape and vanished among the shrubs signified release from the world. There was no vulgar massing of varied bright colours in the landscape garden, for Zen taste required soft, restful tints, while the Japanese gardeners became so skilled that in a few square feet they could create the impression of a quiet, lonely mountain valley. Again there was no attempt to copy nature, for the most powerful effect was produced by a mere suggestion of the atmosphere which Kobori Enshiu described as

> A cluster of summer trees
> A glimpse of the sea,
> A pale evening moon.

As the path drew near to the Tea House a large stone was found by the way, the top of which was hollowed out into a bowl fed with water from a bamboo spout. Here the hands were washed before entering the Tea House, standing at the end of the path in the loneliest part of the garden.

The Spirit of Zen

I look beyond;
Flowers are not,
Nor tinted leaves.
On the sea beach
A solitary cottage stands
In the waning light of an autumn eve.

The House itself was of such fragile structure that at once it suggested the impermanence and emptiness of things; there was no rigidity or formal symmetry in its design, for to Zen symmetry was unnatural and dead, too perfect to leave any room for growth and change, and it was essential that the Tea House should harmonize with its surroundings, that it should be as natural as trees and unhewn rocks. The entrance was so small and low that all who went in had to bow down in humility, while the samurai had to leave his long swords outside. In the tea-room itself there prevailed the same atmosphere of calm and solitude; there was no bright colouring—only the dull yellow of the straw mats and the faint grey of the paper walls, while in the alcove (*tokonoma*) was some masterpiece of Sumiye or Kano painting, or perhaps a rare specimen of calligraphy in plain black and white. Before the picture was set just a solitary branch of blossom or tinted leaves, arranged with infinite care by a hand skilled in the art of flower arrangement. When all the participants were assembled the host would come into the room with the utensils of the ceremony; some of these were rare objects of art which would be passed round for the company's admiration, and in the meantime the tea-kettle would be set to boil on a charcoal brazier. Inside the kettle were placed a few pieces of metal so that the boiling produced a musical sound likened by Kobori Enshiu to 'the soughing of pines on some far away hill, or the sound of a cataract muffled by clouds'. The bowls in which the tea was served were fashioned with the very greatest care, although they appear to be of the roughest workmanship, for the aesthetic ideals of Zen favoured a crude, thick porcelain of a colour resembling the shades of autumn leaves rather than the exquisite 'egg-shell' china adorned with birds and flowers which is so prized by Western collectors. For the object of the tea-ceremony was to make the highest possible use of the simplest materials; it was the Zen monk's reverence for the ordinary things of life carried to its greatest extreme. Thus the participants in the ceremony were expected to appreciate not so much the intrinsic value of the materials used, but the care and artistry with which they had been prepared and arranged. Because the ceremony consisted in an attitude of mind rather than in its utensils, the greatest of all its masters, Sen no Rikyu, said, 'If we have naught but a kettle, we can celebrate the tea-ceremony. Yet there are some who ever insist on the regular utensils, which is foolish.'

In the tea-ceremony we find Zen in its most peaceful aspect, expressed as the highest spiritual freedom and detachment, as an absolute contentment with the natural sufficiency of things. It was an expression of poverty, of separation from earthly belongings, and its basic principles were an insistence on the evanescence of the objective world, a profound love of nature, of her unending changes, her infinite variety, her avoidance of repetition and symmetry, and lastly the indefinable quality called *yugen*, which Mr. Waley has described as 'the subtle, as opposed to the obvious; the hint, as opposed to the statement'. Just as the Koan was a religious device, so *yugen* was an artistic device; it was the method of demonstrating a truth, not by describing it, but by pointing at it so that people might be led to make an immediate contact with life instead of being con-

tent with someone else's version of it. Thus *yugen* was the
'reticence' of Sung and Sumiye paintings—a way of showing
that life can never be fastened down or completely revealed by
the artist's brush, and that there is something ungraspable and
ever elusive to which the painter draws one's attention by the
slightest hint, leaving the rest untouched. A Japanese poet has
said that the means of penetrating *yugen*, of finding out what
it is that lies beneath the surface, is 'to watch the sun sink
behind a flower-clad hill, to wander on and on in a huge forest
without thought of return, to stand upon the shore and gaze
after a boat that goes hid by far-off islands, to ponder on the
journey of wild geese seen and lost among the clouds'. Somehow these words seem to contain the whole spirit of the tea-
ceremony, for the feelings which they express lie at the root
of Chinese and Japanese aesthetics as influenced by Zen; they
have that strange, haunting beauty, that atmosphere of complete freedom from care, which has made the Cult of Tea
recognized throughout Japan as the supreme method of bringing rest and quietness to the mind and refreshment and insight
to the spirit.

Yet the artistic ideals of Zen may very easily degenerate into
sentimentalism, especially when the 'quietistic' aspect is
accepted without the 'dynamic' aspect, which is expressed in
the military arts. The danger is in regarding *yugen* as an end
in itself, rather than as a means of discovering a deeper secret.
The aesthetic technique of Zen is no more the essential reality
than its religious technique of Koans, smacks on the face and
abrupt remarks. Many writers have sentimentalized over the
'simple life' of the Zen monk and his taste for unadorned,
suggestive and unobtrusive things, but that is a life seen from
the outside. No understanding of Zen could be obtained from
the tea-ceremony if it were not accompanied by work in the

monastery, for there was nothing sentimental about the masters who used to box their disciples' ears to bring them to their senses, and who experienced life 'close to Nature' not only when she was warm and pleasant but when she was freezing, wet and stormy. The sentimental 'lover of Nature' only sees one side of her face; when it is wet he goes indoors or puts up his umbrella and speaks of the delightful hissing of the rain on the leaves. He does not let it trickle down his neck.

If anyone suspects Zen of sentimentalism, his suspicions will be swiftly set at rest by a consideration of the life of the Samurai. In sharp contrast to the quietism of the Cult of Tea, Zen becomes fierce and stormy when it is expressed in *ju-jutsu* and *kenjutsu*, although there is still an underlying calm which, however, resembles the solidity of a mighty rock rather than poetical detachment. *Ju-jutsu* or *judo* means literally 'the gentle art', and while *ju-jutsu* is specifically the technique of locks, strangles and throws, *judo* is rather the philosophy upon which this technique is based, while the same distinction is made between *kenjutsu* and *kendo*. *Ju-jutsu* is a method of self-defence without weapons founded on the principle of defeating one's opponent by yielding to him and using his own strength. Its origins will be found in the philosophy of *wu-wei*, and according to a legend it was first discovered through watching the snow fall on the branches of trees. On the branches of tough and rigid trees the snow piles up until they crack beneath its weight, while thin and springy branches simply yield and throw it to the ground without being broken or bent. Thus Lao Tzu says:

> Man at his birth is tender and weak; at his death he is rigid and strong. . . . Thus rigidity and strength are the concomitants of death; softness and weakness are the concomitants of life.
>
> (*Trans.* LIONEL GILES.)

115

Ju-jutsu is founded on the two principles of *wu-wei* and 'going right ahead' or immediacy of attack and defence. *Wu-wei* as applied to *ju-jutsu* may be illustrated by the analogy of a bar of wood revolving about its central point of balance. If one strikes it on either side of the centre it will swing away, and the only chance of knocking it off its balance will be to hit straight at the centre. But imagine a bar of wood which can move itself at will, and which is therefore capable of moving its centre out of the line of an oncoming force. However much one may strike at it, it will just shift its centre out of the direct line of one's blows and so make its weakness its strength. In the case of the human body the central point of balance is at the pit of the stomach; any attack made above that point is made ineffectual by bending away from it, while an attack to the side is avoided by stepping slightly out of the direct line and pivoting in such a way as to let it pass. But the human body is unlike the bar of wood in so far as it has to stand with one end on the ground; therefore an attack below the point of balance is invariably successful unless both feet are placed firmly on the ground with the pit of the stomach supported evenly above them, neither too far forward nor too far back. In this position the legs are slightly bent at the knees to afford a certain amount of 'give', and anyone skilled in *ju-jutsu* will maintain this position for as long as possible, moving with his feet always the same distance apart (directly under the shoulders) and never raising them more than a fraction of an inch from the ground. Attack in *ju-jutsu* is effected by manœuvring one's opponent until his balance becomes unsteady; this may happen in two ways. Either he will make a false step so that the body is not supported evenly by the feet, and in this event he can be thrown easily to the ground by a sharp sideways blow on one or other of his ankles; or else he will unbalance himself by making an attack, and in this case the defender will simply swing away on his own point of balance, causing the force of the attack to overstep itself by finding no resistance. And then, by pulling the attacking limb in the direction in which it was aimed, or by pushing at a part of the attacker's body on the opposite side of his point of balance to the part with which he attacked, he is rendered as powerless as a falling tree.

Therefore the more force one uses in trying to defeat an expert in *ju-jutsu*, the more one is likely to be hurt. It is like barging heavily against a door with a weak latch; it simply flies open and throws one to the floor. In this way the exponent of *ju-jutsu* is like life itself; try to catch hold of him or to strike him down so that he has no more power over you, and he is no longer there. The more you struggle, and the harder you hit, the faster he slips away, for he is so poised that you actually push him away with your own strength.

Coming to the second principle—immediacy of attack and defence—we find that there can be no success in *ju-jutsu* if there is even the slightest interval between these two movements. If one stops to think out a counter-move for a fraction of a second, one's opponent has time to regain his balance, for it is precisely by yielding correctly to his attack *as he makes it* that he is defeated. If the yielding is at all late he finds just enough resistance to prevent his attack from overstepping itself, and the moment he finds something which he can fight *against* he has a chance of success. The essence of *ju-jutsu* is that there should never be anything which can be fought against; the expert must be as elusive as the truth of Zen; he must make himself into a Koan—a puzzle which slips away the more one tries to solve it; he must be like water in that he falls through the fingers of those who try to clutch him. Water does not hesitate before it yields, for the moment the fingers begin to close it moves away, not of its own strength, but by using the pressure applied to it. Therefore in *ju-jutsu* the two combatants move as one man; attack and defence is one movement, and there is no straining, no resistance and no hesitation, until with a sudden thud one of the men seems to have been hurled to the ground with gigantic force. He has made a false step, and his opponent has thrown him off his balance so that he falls with the full force of his own weight, with perhaps just an extra push from behind to add speed to his defeat.

Somewhat similar principles are applied in *kenjutsu*—the art of fencing with a bamboo substitute for the Samurai's long, two-handed sword with a single edge so sharp that it can cleave a man's body from the collar-bone to the centre of his chest. *Wu-wei* is not so much in evidence here as in *ju-jutsu*, although immediacy of attack and defence is again a principle of supreme importance. As before, the pit of the stomach is made the centre of activity, and cuts are delivered not so much with the arms as with this central point of balance using the arms as its levers. Thus in making a cut at the top of the opponent's head the arms are stiff and rigid at the moment of impact, the force being derived from a sudden forward movement of the whole body. As this movement is made, and throughout the whole combat, the fencer must move as from the pit of his stomach, using it as a firm pivot upon which the rest of the body can be swung instantly to the right or to the left as occasion requires. Here again we have the principle of the calm centre in the midst of lightning activity; throughout the quick cuts and parries the point of balance must remain as far as possible unmoved. There is no violent jumping from side to side or running backwards and forwards, for in *kenjutsu* there must be no waste of energy. Therefore the source of strength and the centre of action is kept still until the moment comes for a deathly blow, and then the blade is brought down with a terrific sweep, ending in a swift and powerful forward movement of the centre, accompanied with a tremendous shout, made as if the breath were being forced up from the depths of the stomach.

The mental attitude of the fencer must be what is known as the state of *Muga*—that is, an absence of the feeling that 'I am doing it'. This feeling is held to be a great hindrance since just as in listening to music the concept of oneself listening or oneself fencing draws the attention away from the melody or from the actual movements of the swords. The consciousness of 'self' must be subordinated to concentration on the task in hand, and the mind must follow the opponent's movements so closely and respond to them so immediately that once more the dualism of 'attack' and 'defence' becomes a unity. It was this attitude of mind that lay at the heart of *bushido*—the 'Way of the Warrior'. In feudal Japan internal wars between rival barons (*daimyo*) were frequent events, and warriors went in constant danger of their lives. It was the 'straightforwardness' of Zen that preserved their mental stability, and the Samurai would make frequent visits to the Zen masters that they might gather strength from the religion of 'going right ahead with no looking back', which taught that life and death were but aspects of the same existence, and which showed how 'self' might be forgotten in its unity with life. *Bushido* required unquestioning loyalty to one's lord and master, great physical courage and fortitude, and above all this attitude of *Muga* which is described in what is known as the Samurai's creed:

I have no parents; I make heaven and earth my parents.
I have no divine power; I make honesty my power.
I have no means; I make submission my means.

The Spirit of Zen

I have no magic power; I make inward strength my magic.
I have neither life nor death; I make the Eternal my life and death.
I have no body; I make fortitude my body.
I have no eyes; I make the flash of lightning my eyes.
I have no ears; I make sensibility my ears.
I have no limbs; I make promptitude my limbs.
I have no design; I make opportunity my design.
I have no miracles; I make the Dharma my miracle.
I have no principles; I make adaptability to all things my principles.
I have no friends; I make my mind my friend.
I have no enemy; I make incautiousness my enemy.
I have no armour; I make goodwill and righteousness my armour.
I have no castle; I make immovable mind my castle.
I have no sword; I make 'the sleep of the mind' my sword.

Conclusion

The history of Zen and of the way in which it has moulded the whole culture of the Far East would require a special volume to itself. The purpose of this book has been simply to give a clue to the spirit of Zen and to outline some of the ways in which it has been translated into thought and action. In writing about Zen there are two extremes to be avoided: the one to define and explain so little that the reader is completely bewildered, and the other to define and explain so much that the reader thinks he understands Zen! Throughout it has been emphasized that Zen is an immediate contact with life, a joining of 'self' and 'life' into so close a unity and rhythm that the distinction between the two is forgotten, that the desire to possess is abandoned because there is nothing that can possess and nothing that can be possessed. The isolated 'self' no longer wishes to grasp at the things which flow by in the stream of events, for it goes forward with the stream and becomes one with it, realizing that all things are but waves in this stream and that to try to clutch hold of them is to make them disappear. From this it might seem that Zen can be defined as the unity of man and the universe, as the rhythm of the mind with changing forms, as a state of 'One-ness' in which all distinctions of 'I' and 'not-I', knower and known, seer and seen, are set aside. And yet master Tao-wu said, 'Even One-ness when held on to is wide of the mark.'

For the truth is that in Zen as in life there is nothing at all which one can hold on to and say, 'This is it; I have got it.' Therefore any book about Zen is rather like a mystery story

Conclusion

with the last chapter missing; there is always something which escapes definition, which can never be expressed in words, and however hard we may try to catch up with it, it is always one pace ahead. But this is because definition and description is death, and the truth of Zen can no more be killed than the many-headed dragon of the ancient myth which always grew another head as soon as one was cut off. For Zen is life; to chase after Zen is like chasing one's own shadow, and all the time one is running away from the sun. When at last it is realized that the shadow can never be caught, there is a sudden 'turning about', a flash of satori, and in the light of the sun the dualism of self and its shadow vanishes; whereat man perceives that what he was chasing was only the unreal image of the one true Self—of That which he ever was, is and shall be. At last he has found Enlightenment.

125

126

128

129

Glossary

AVIDYA: (Sanskrit). Ignorance or self-delusion; belief in the duality of 'self' and the external world, as distinct from the realization that both are aspects of the same 'Buddha-nature,' which is the one true Self.

BODHI: (Sanskrit). Enlightenment, the opposite of *Avidya*.

DHARMA: (Sanskrit). This word has many shades of meaning. The nearest English equivalent is 'Law,' and the three most important meanings are: the fundamental Law upon which all the processes of life are based, the way in which the universe works; the Law or Teaching of the Buddha; as applied to each separate thing, the law of its being, its function.

KARMA: (Sanskrit). Its literal meaning is 'action' and from this it has come to mean the law conditioning action which is cause and effect. *Karma* does not mean 'Fate,' except in the sense that man cannot escape from the effects of his own deeds, though so far as the deeds themselves are concerned he is free to choose. A person's *karma* is thus the destiny which falls to him as a result of his own actions—in other words, the circumstances under which he lives.

NIRVANA: (Sanskrit). Release from Samsara (q.v.). The spiritual freedom attained by realizing one's identity with the 'Buddha-nature' enables one to be free from *karma*, for the 'Buddha-nature' cannot be conditioned by any form of action. This freedom from *karma* makes it possible to enter into eternal rest since the effects of one's deeds can no longer draw one back to the world (*v.* Rebirth). If one chooses to enter the world no more, then Nirvana is entered.

REBIRTH: The corollary of *karma*. The doctrine that each individual is born into the world again and again to inherit the effects of his deeds, or rather, that by action in this life the individual creates a fresh personality for himself in order that the results of his actions may be fulfilled in a future life.

SAMSARA: (Sanskrit). The alternation of birth and death, sometimes called the Wheel of Birth and Death. This is explained by reference to the other alternating processes of life—day and night, waking and sleeping, the seasons, etc. Death is only a pause for rest in the life-process of the individual and arises because his physical body is worn out. But this wearing out does not imply the end of his life-process, and new bodies are created in order that he may continue to work out his *karma*.

SUNYATA: (Sanskrit). The emptiness of all separate things as such. The only abiding principle in life is the 'Buddha-nature,' which manifests itself in separate forms. These forms have no permanence or reality as forms, only as 'Buddha-nature.' For this reason Mahayana philosophy declares that they are empty.

YOGA: (Sanskrit). Literally a yoke or discipline; the technique of meditation whereby the individual brings himself into unity with the Ultimate Reality of the universe. There are four types of Yoga, representing the four paths to this union—Gnana, the path of Knowledge, Karma, the path of Action, Bhakti, the path of Love, and Raja, the Royal Path which is a synthesis of the other three. A fifth and debased type of Yoga is Hatha, consisting of complicated physical and psychic exercises—a spiritual *cul-de-sac*, which, if undertaken without the greatest care, is apt to have dangerous results.

Bibliography

ANESAKI, M. *History of Japanese Religion.* Kegan Paul, London, 1930.

BENOIT, H. *The Supreme Doctrine.* Pantheon, New York, and Routledge, London, 1955.

BLOFELD, J. *The Path to Sudden Attainment.* Buddhist Society, London, 1948.

The Zen Teaching of Huang Po. Rider, London, 1958.

BLYTH, R. L. *Zen in English Literature and Oriental Classics.* Hokuseido, Tokyo, 1948.

Haiku. 4 vols. Hokuseido, Tokyo, 1952.

Buddhist Sermons on Christian Texts. Tokyo, 1952.

DUMOULIN, H. 'Die Entwicklung des chinesischen Ch'an.' *Monumenta Serica,* 1941, IV.

'Das Wu-men-kuan oder "Der Pass ohne Tor."' *Monumenta Serica,* 1943, VIII.

'Bodhidharma und die Anfänge des Ch'an Buddhismus.' *Monumenta Nipponica,* 1951, VII.

DUMOULIN, H. & SASAKI, R. F. *The Development of Chinese Zen after the Sixth Patriarch.* First Zen Institute, New York, 1953.

ELIOT, SIR CHARLES. *Japanese Buddhism.* Arnold, London, 1935.

FUNG, YU-LAN. *A History of Chinese Philosophy.* 2 vols. trs. Derk Bodde. Princeton, 1953.

The Spirit of Chinese Philosophy. trs. E. R. Hughes. Kegan Paul, London, 1947.

GATENBY, E. V. *The Cloud Men of Yamato.* Murray, London, 1929.

GERNET, J. 'Entretiens du Maître de Dhyana Chen-houei du Ho-tsö.' *Bulletin de l'École Française d'Extrême-Orient,* 1949, XXXI.

'Biographie du Maître Chen-houei de Ho-tsö.' *Journal Asiatique,* 1951.

'Entretiens du Maître Ling-yeou du Kouei-chan.' *Bulletin de l'École Française d'Extrême-Orient,* 1951, XLV, 1.

GROSSE, E. *Die Ostasiatische Tuschmalerei.* Cassirer, Berlin, 1923.

The Spirit of Zen

HARRISON, E. J. *The Fighting Spirit of Japan*. Unwin, London, 1913.

HERRIGEL, E. *Zen in the Art of Archery*. Pantheon, New York, 1953; Routledge & Kegan Paul, London, 1953.

HUMPHREYS, C. *Zen Buddhism*. Allen & Unwin, London, 1958.

HU SHIH. 'The Development of Zen Buddhism in China.' *Chinese Political and Social Review*, 1932, XV, 4.

NUKARIYA, K. *The Religion of the Samurai*. Luzac, London, 1913.

OGATA, S. *Guide to Zen Practice*. A translation of the Mu-mon-kwan. Bukkasha, Kyoto, 1934.

OHASAMA, S. & FAUST, A. *Zen, der lebendige Buddhismus in Japan*. Gotha, 1925.

OKAKURA, K. *The Book of Tea*. Foulis, Edinburgh, 1919.

SASAKI, SOKEI-AN. (ed.) *Cat's Yawn*. First Zen Institute of America, New York, 1947.

SENZAKI, N. *Zen Meditation*. Bukkasha, Kyoto, 1936.

SENZAKI, N. & REPS, P. *Zen Flesh, Zen Bones*. Tuttle, Tokyo, and Rutland, Vermont, 1957.

SENZAKI, N. & McCANDLESS, R. *Buddhism and Zen*. Philosophical Library, New York, 1953.

SHAKU, SOYEN. *Sermons of a Buddhist Abbot*. Open Court, Chicago, 1906.

SOGEN, ASAHINA. *Zen*. Sakane, Tokyo, 1954.

STEINILBER-OBERLIN, E. & MATSUO, K. *The Buddhist Sects of Japan*. Allen & Unwin, London, 1938.

SUZUKI, B. L. *Mahayana Buddhism*. Marlowe, London, 1948.

SUZUKI, D. T. *Essays in Zen Buddhism*. 3 vols. Luzac, London, 1927, 1933, 1934. Reprinted, Rider, London, 1949, 1950, 1951.

Studies in the Lankavatara Sutra. Routledge, London 1957.

Introduction to Zen Buddhism. Rider, London, 1949.

Training of the Zen Buddhist Monk. Eastern Buddhist Society, Kyoto, 1934.

Manual of Zen Buddhism. Kyoto, 1935. Repr. Rider, London, 1950.

Zen and Japanese Culture. Pantheon, New York, 1958. (A revision of the Japanese edition of 1938.)

The Essence of Buddhism. Buddhist Society, London, 1947.

The Zen Doctrine of No-Mind. Rider, London, 1949.

Living by Zen. Rider, London, 1950.

Mysticism: Christian and Buddhist. Harper, New York, 1957.

Studies in Zen. Rider, London, 1955.

Bibliography

'Ignorance and World Fellowship.' *Faiths and Fellowship*. Watkins, London, 1937.

'An Interpretation of Zen Experience.' *Philosophy, East and West*, ed. Charles Moore. Princeton, 1944.

'Buddhist Symbolism.' *Symbols and Values*. Harper, New York, 1954.

'Zen and Pragmatism.' *Philosophy, East and West*. Honolulu, 1954, IV, 2.

TAKAKUSU, J. *Essentials of Buddhist Philosophy*. University of Hawaii, Honolulu, 1947.

WALEY, A. *Zen Buddhism and Its Relation to Art*. Luzac, London, 1922.

WATTS, A. W. *Zen Buddhism*. Buddhist Society, London, 1947.

Zen. (Same as above, but enlarged.) Delkin, Stanford, 1948.

The Way of Zen. Pantheon, New York, and Thames & Hudson, London, 1957.

WONG, MOU-LAM. *The Sutra of Wei Lang*. Luzac, London, 1944.

List of Illustrations

The Spirit of Zen

Selected Grove Press Paperbacks

B60	BRECHT, BERTOLT / Baal, A Man's A Man, The Elephant Calf / $1.95
B312	BRECHT, BERTOLT / The Caucasian Chalk Circle / $1.95
B414	BRECHT, BERTOLT / The Mother / $2.95
B108	BRECHT, BERTOLT / Mother Courage and Her Children / $1.95
E580	BRETON, ANDRE / Nadja / $3.95
E751	BROWN, DEENA, ed. / American Yoga / $9.95
B193	BULGAKOV, MIKHAIL / The Heart of a Dog / $2.95
B147	BULGAKOV, MIKHAIL / The Master and Margarita / $3.95
B115	BURROUGHS, WILLIAM / Naked Lunch / $2.95
B446	BURROUGHS, WILLIAM / The Soft Machine, Nova Express, The Wild Boys: Three Novels / $4.95
B147	BURROUGHS, WILLIAM / The Ticket That Exploded / $2.95
B440	CLEVE, JOHN / The Crusader: Books I and II / $2.95
E773	CLURMAN, HAROLD, ed. / Nine Plays of the Modern Theater (Waiting for Godot by Samuel Beckett, The Visit by Friedrich Dürrenmatt, Tango by Slawomir Mrozek, The Caucasian Chalk Circle by Bertolt Brecht, The Balcony by Jean Genet, Rhinoceros by Eugéne Ionesco, American Buffalo by David Mamet, The Birthday Party by Harold Pinter, and Rosencrantz and Guildenstern are Dead by Tom Stoppard) / $9.50
E771	COCTEAU / Jean / Opium: The Diary of a Cure / $5.95
B405	CRAFTS, KATHY and HAUTHER, BRENDA / The Student's Guide to Good Grades / $2.45
E739	CROCKETT, JIM, ed. / The Guitar Player Book (Revised and Updated Edition) / $9.95
E190	CUMMINGS, E. E. / 100 Selected Poems / $1.95
E159	DELANEY, SHELAGH / A Taste of Honey / $3.95
E639	DOSS, MARGARET PATTERSON / San Francisco at Your Feet (Second Revised Edition) / $4.95
B412	DOYLE, RODGER and REDDING, JAMES / The Complete Food Handbook. Revised and Updated ed. / $3.50
B75	DURAS, MARGUERITE / Four Novels (The Afternoon of Mr. Andesmas, 10:30 On a Summer Night, Moderato Cantabile, The Square) / $3.95
E284	DURAS, MARGUERITE / Hiroshima Mon Amour. Text for the Film by Alain Resnais. Illus. / $3.95
E380	DURRENMATT, FRIEDRICH / The Physicists / $2.95
E344	DURRENMATT, FRIEDRICH / The Visit / $2.95
B179	FANON, FRANTZ / Black Skin, White Masks / $2.95

E216	KEENE, DONALD, ed. / Anthology of Japanese Literature: Earliest Era to Mid-19th Century / $5.95
E573	KEENE, DONALD, ed. / Modern Japanese Literature: An Anthology / $7.95
E522	KEROUAC, JACK / Mexico City Blues / $3.95
B300	KEROUAC, JACK / The Subterraneans / $1.95
E705	KERR, CARMEN / Sex For Women Who Want To Have Fun and Loving Relationships With Equals / $4.95
E492	KOLAKOWSKI, LESZEK / Toward a Marxist Humanism / $3.95
B413	LAVERTY, FRANK / The O.K. Way To Slim / $2.95
B9	LAWRENCE, D. H. / Lady Chatterley's Lover / $1.95
B335	LEGMAN, G. / Rationale of the Dirty Joke / $2.95
E748	LESSER, MICHAEL, M.D. / Nutrition and Vitamin Therapy / $7.95
B262	LESTER, JULIUS / Black Folktales / $2.95
E163	LEWIS, MATTHEW / The Monk / $5.95
E578	LINSSEN, ROBERT / Living Zen / $3.95
E54	LORCA, FEDERICO / Poet in New York. Bilingual ed. / $4.95
B373	LUCAS, GEORGE / American Graffiti / $1.75
E701	MALRAUX, ANDRE / The Conquerors / $3.95
E719	MALRAUX, ANDRE / Lazarus / $2.95
E697	MAMET, DAVID / American Buffalo / $3.95
E709	MAMET, DAVID / A Life in the Theatre / $3.95
E716	MAMET, DAVID / The Water Engine and Mr. Happiness / $3.95
B326	MILLER HENRY / Nexus / $2.95
B100	MILLER HENRY / Plexus / $3.95
B325	MILLER HENRY / Sexus / $3.95
B10	MILLER, HENRY / Tropic of Cancer / $2.50
B59	MILLER, HENRY / Tropic of Capricorn / $1.95
E583	MISHIMA, YUKIO / Sun and Steel / $3.95
E433	MROZEK, SLAWOMIR / Tango / $3.95
E568	MROZEK, SLAWOMIR / Vatzlav / $1.95
E770	NELSON, PAUL / Rod Stewart: A Biography / $8.95
E636	NERUDA, PABLO / Five Decades: Poems 1925–1970. Bilingual ed. / $5.95
E364	NERUDA, PABLO / Selected Poems. Bilingual ed. / $5.95
E650	NICHOLS, PETER / The National Health / $3.95
B199	OE, KENZABURO / A Personal Matter / $3.95
E687	OE, KENZABURO / Teach Us To Outgrow Our Madness / $4.95
E413	O'HARA, FRANK / Meditations in an Emergency / $4.95

B433   SAUNERON, SERGE / The Priests of Ancient Egypt / $3.50

E395   SHATTUCK, ROGER, and TAYLOR, SIMON WATSON, eds. / Selected Works of Alfred Jarry / $6.95

E684   STOPPARD, TOM / Dirty Linen and New-Found-Land / $2.95

E703   STOPPARD, TOM / Every Good Boy Deserves Favor and Professional Foul: Two Plays / $3.95

E489   STOPPARD, TOM / The Real Inspector Hound and After Magritte: Two Plays / $3.95

B319   STOPPARD, TOM / Rosencrantz and Guildenstern Are Dead / $1.95

E341   SUZUKI, D. T. / Introduction to Zen Buddhism / $1.95

E231   SUZUKI, D. T. / Manual of Zen Buddhism / $3.95

E749   THELWELL, MICHAEL / The Harder They Come / $7.95

B432   TROCCHI, ALEXANDER / Cain's Book / $3.50

E658   TRUFFAUT, FRANCOIS / Day for Night / $3.95

B399   TRUFFAUT, FRANCOIS / Small Change / $1.95

B395   TRUFFAUT, FRANCOIS / The Story of Adele H / $2.45

E699   TURGENEV, IVAN / Virgin Soil / $3.95

E328   TUTUOLA, AMOS / The Palm-Wine Drinkard / $2.45

E414   VIAN, BORIS / The Empire Builders / $2.95

E746   VITHOULKAS, GEORGE / The Science of Homeopathy / $9.50

E209   WALEY, ARTHUR, Jr. / The Book of Songs / $5.95

E84   WALEY, ARTHUR / The Way and Its Power: A Study of the Tao Te Ching and its Place in Chinese Thought / $4.95

E689   WALKENSTEIN, EILEEN / Don't Shrink to Fit! A Confrontation With Dehumanization in Psychiatry and Psychology / $3.95

E579   WARNER, LANGDON / The Enduring Art of Japan / $4.95

B365   WARNER, SAMUEL J. / Self Realization and Self Defeat / $2.95

E219   WATTS, ALAN W. / The Spirit of Zen / $2.95

E112   WU, CH'ENG-EN / Monkey / $4.95

E767   WYCKOFF, HOGIE / Solving Problems Together / $7.95

E688   WYCKOFF, HOGIE / Solving Women's Problems Through Awareness, Action and Contact / $4.95

B106   YU, LI / Jou Pu Tuan / $1.95

GROVE PRESS, INC., 196 West Houston St., New York, N.Y. 10014